TEARFUL *Surrender* JOYFUL *Release*

Journey From Brokenness
to Breakthrough

MARQUITA E. BATCHELOR

© 2014 Marquita E. Batchelor

TEARFUL *Surrender,* JOYFUL *Release*
Journey from Brokenness to Breakthrough

Printed in the USA
Library of Congress Control Number: 2014949072
ISBN (Print): 978-0-9907314-0-5
ISBN (Kindle): 978-0-9907314-1-2
ISBN (eBook): 978-0-9907314-2-9

Prepared for Publication by Palm Tree Publications, a Division of Palm Tree Productions
WWW.PALMTREEPRODUCTIONS.COM

To Contact the Author:

MARQUITA *E*.COM

DEDICATION

TO MY MOTHER

You have always been there for me. Growing up, you would often tell me you were the best friend I would ever have in this world. Being young and naïve, I did not believe you, but like so many other things in life, I found out you were right. God blessed me with you, the best mother in the world, a godly mother, a praying mother, a giving and nurturing mother.

Through the darkest days of my life and some of my most painful experiences, you were with me and for me. Every day without fail you told me that God was faithful and would bring me through every test and trial. You encouraged me with scriptures, your wise counsel, and I knew you were praying for me. Just as you had done when I was a little girl, you gave me food, brought me clothes, gave me money, and helped to keep a roof over my head. You did whatever you could within your power to ease my pain.

You once told me that watching me live through the most difficult times in my life hurt you more than it hurt me. You would often tell us this when you had to discipline us and I never believed it then. But this was different—somehow I felt you really did agonize and hurt as much as I did.

One of your favorite scriptures is Proverbs 22:6, "Train up a child in the way he should go and when he is old, he will not depart from it." You taught me that regardless of how people treated us, what they said about us, or what they did to us, we were not to return evil for evil. You engrained in my spiritual DNA that I was not responsible for other's actions but God would hold me accountable for mine. I credit your teachings for being one of the reasons why I was able to suffer in silence, not retaliate, and live to see God's vindication.

Mom, I thank God for your unconditional love and for the rich spiritual heritage you have given me. I honor you with this, my first book, and I will always love you.

—MARQUITA *E.*

WHAT OTHERS ARE SAYING

"After traveling to destinations with Marquita such as England and South Africa, I have found her to be a student and great teacher of the Word of God. She has the ability to make the digestion of the Word easy and applicable. An adaptable person, she is prepared to serve in any place. Her ability to minister the Gospel to people, especially women is tremendous. The anointing and the call on her life are evident.

"I am excited to see the new and dynamic things God has placed before her to do. I celebrate the completion of this wonderful book, *Tearful Surrender, Joyful Release*. I know it will be an encouragement to you."

—PASTOR CONNIE BROOKS
Jubilee International Ministries, Pittsburgh, PA

"I have known Marquita as a woman of purpose and tenacity who carries the presence of God with dignity and reverence. She ministered with much power at the Born to Reign Conference in Johannesburg, South Africa, co-hosted by Marketplace Calling International. *Tearful Surrender* has the same power to impact and change lives because it is Marquita's story and her life is filled with surrender to God and a deep desire to walk worthy of His call.

— DR. ZIENZILE MUSAMIRAPAMWE
Founder, Marketplace Calling International (MCI)

"Marquita has been a wonderful part of the vision of New Spirit Revival Center for the last fourteen years. I call her daughter and friend. In *Tearful Surrender, Joyful Release* you will read about what I have personally witnessed as Marquita goes from happiness, through periods of grief and sadness, and then on to victory. She is a powerful vessel in the Kingdom of God and great things have come out of Marquita's life as the anointing has increased in her more and more. Everyone she touches is blessed and I have no doubt as you allow her to touch you through *Tearful Surrender, Joyful Release*, you will be immensely blessed as well."

—DR. BELINDA SCOTT
Co-Pastor, New Spirit Revival Center
Cleveland Heights, Ohio

ACKNOWLEDGEMENTS

- God First— *for His unfailing love, for His faithfulness, and for always being there with me.*

- My brother and sister-in-love, Jonathan and Sharon Robinson— *my number 2 and 3 supporters and fans (after Mom). I love you to life.*

- My best friends, Marlene Moore, Jewel Thomas, and Gayle Cook—*Tried and true, you did not disappoint.*

- My pastors, Darrell and Belinda Scott—*for preaching me through the storms.*

- Wendy K. Walters—*for coaching me through to the completion of my first book.*

"For I know the plans I have for you," says the Lord. "They are plans for good and not for disaster, to give you a future and a hope."
—JEREMIAH 29:11, NLT

CONTENTS

"Those who sow in tears will reap with songs of joy."
—PSALM 126:5, NIV

FOREWORD
BY DR. MARK CHIRONNA

I met Marquita in 1986 at the opening of The Lord's Church in Monroeville, Pennsylvania. It was the first time I preached for my dear friend, Pastor Archie Dennis Jr., and Marquita and her best friend Niecy (Archie's daughter) introduced themselves to me together. They were both radiant—with a sense of boundless joy and love for Jesus, it was infectious! My first impression of her was connected to the gleam in her bright eyes, the compelling smile on her face, and the warmth in her voice. She struck me as a most resilient and hopeful person, a woman of integrity who carried herself with great dignity and grace. She was part of the new family of friends I was making in Pittsburgh, and I was honored to get to know her.

Marquita's transparency and authenticity have always touched me deeply, and I have the highest respect and regard for her as a friend and a woman of God. My journey took me from Pittsburgh to North Carolina, and ultimately to Orlando. Hers led from Pittsburgh to Cleveland (with my precious friends the Scotts), and we have stayed in touch throughout the years.

All of us experience "rites of passage" in our life, and some of those take us into what theologians refer to as "liminal space." Liminal space is that place where we cross a threshold and a significant transformation happens in relation to all things sacred. It is a place filled with times of tension, extreme reactions, and great opportunity. Scripture refers to this as a "fullness of times."

When Elijah and Elisha cross the Jordan at the time of Elijah's departure the chariots of Israel divide them. Elisha cries out both in awe and in grief as the chariots reveal the invisible world to him and yet simultaneously separate him from his mentor as Elijah is caught up into the chariot. Liminal space can be entered in seasons of grief (though not exclusively) when the world behind the veil of this illusion of permanence we call "reality" becomes quite thin, and someone we love passes beyond that veil to the greater reality of what C.S. Lewis referred to as the "Unseen Real."

God uses grief as a doorway to newness, yet it isn't an easy space to navigate. I remember learning that Marquita was getting married and I was excited for her. A few years later I received word that her husband was not doing well, and as things unfolded he eventually crossed that veil between this reality and that greater reality with Marquita by his side. That beautiful transparency and authenticity I mentioned earlier is evident in the pages of *Tearful Surrender, Joyful Release* and you get to experience and connect with Marquita on the printed page in the same way that those of us who love and value her have gotten to know her up close and personally.

You can't read this story of her journey without recognizing her humanness, tenderness, realness, and readiness to pursue God—even when it is painful. Her love for Jesus shines on every page, as does her love for family, husband, friends, and life itself. This book is a piece of her heart and a journey through her pain in liminal space as a gift to you, dear reader, so that from her pain, you can find great promise and hope.

That old Sunday School chorus, "Jesus Loves Me This I Know" is true. You can't read this story and not know that. Let Marquita take you by the hand and lead you into the Presence of the One who is the Lover of your soul. Give yourself permission to shed tears with her; they will be cathartic and healing. I commend you into her able hands.

—BISHOP MARK J. CHIRONNA, MA, PH.D.
Mark Chironna Ministries
Church On The Living Edge
Orlando, Florida

You keep track of all my sorrows,
You have collected all my tears in your bottle.
You have recorded each one in your book.
—PSALM 56:8, NLT

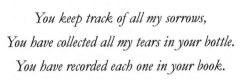

PREFACE

I have often said, "Life happens to us all."

Whether you live life at a steady, manageable pace as I prefer, or you live life fast and furious, one situation can change you forever. Suddenly and without notice, you could find yourself in the thralls of the most challenging circumstances.

What do you do when everything in your world turns upside down and inside out? Out of nowhere, a life crisis blindsides you, throws your whole world out of sync, and sends you spiraling downward in a tailspin. What do you do when you cannot find employment or lose a home? What happens if your spouse is diagnosed with a life-threatening disease? Any one of these events alone could easily rock your world, and disrupt your balance. This is the exact situation I found myself in.

I have known I had to write this book for several years. For any number of reasons, I would start writing and then stop. Because I am a private person, sharing my emotions, thoughts, and perceptions about personal difficulties and challenges in my life is something I've always reserved for my closest friends. Reflecting on past hurts conjured up a well of fresh tears. Reliving painful events caused all of the emotions that I had long since thought were gone to surface as though it happened yesterday. Perhaps my biggest challenge to writing surrounds some of the people involved in my story. I hold them in high regard and I still respect them in spite of hurtful actions. This is not a tell-all. I have no interest in casting anyone in a disparaging light. This is my story. My memoir. My journey.

I have finally resolved within myself that I have a story worth telling. If I must write through tears in order for my healing to be complete, then that's what I will do. Others need to know that no matter what life brings, God will always be there with them … as He was with me.

TO MOVE FORWARD I MUST FIRST GO BACK

To move forward I must first go back. I must honestly recount days filled with misunderstandings, deception, disappointment, and ultimately, God's vindication and restoration.

I always knew that one day I would write this book. Realizing how quickly memories fade, where possible I kept emails and other documents to verify facts. Many of the events and conversations contained in these pages are based on my memories and may not be the way others recall them.

Throughout this journey, there have been many tests, trials, and triumphs, but most importantly, there has been a tearful surrender to God's will and purpose for my life.

Chapter One

SINGLE AND SATISFIED

Single and satisfied! I finally reached a place in my life where I fully embraced being single. I was content as a single women. Actually, I've come to this place twice in my lifetime. The first time was before I married, and it took many years before I was comfortable as a party of one. The second time was after becoming widowed. Arriving at the place of satisfaction, in either instance, did not come quickly and was not an easy journey.

I grew up in Clairton, a small steel town in western Pennsylvania. Like most girls at that time, I did not expect to be a career woman. Two income households were not the norm then. My dream was to be an executive secretary right up until I could become a wife and mother. I was socialized to grow up, get married, and raise a family. My childhood was spent practicing for the inevitable. I spent hours playing house and playing with baby dolls.

My father, a social worker at the Pennsylvania department of Public Assistance, did not feel there would be a return on his investment if he sent me to college. I told him he was a male chauvinist and I learned quickly that he did not like my comment when I felt the back of his hand swish across my mouth. In spite of that, I know he would have been the proud father had he lived to see me graduate with a master's degree in hand.

My father's views were not uncommon. We lived in a couples-oriented culture which made single and satisfied sound like an oxymoron. The music, movies, magazines, and commercials, all pointed towards having that special someone to fill the void in an otherwise lonely life.

EXISTING SINGLE

Being single can make you feel like a second class citizen with a plague or some kind of dreadful disease. Questions like, "Why are you still single?" and "Why aren't you married yet?" seemed to be a part of every conversation. Whether the questions came from well meaning family and friends or someone who was deliberately being mean, something would pierce my heart like a dagger. What do you say? How do you answer? Whatever I said in response was simply to deflect the conversation elsewhere and mask my true feelings.

I became a master at masking my feelings—even from myself. The unmasking didn't come until much later. Ben Franklin once said, "There are three things extremely hard: steel, a diamond, and to know one's self."

On the road to becoming single and satisfied, discovering my identity was one of the most important things that ever happened to me. It took me a very long time to evolve; a process much like a furry, creepy, caterpillar transforming into a colorful, beautiful butterfly, or an ugly duckling into an elegant and graceful swan.

At an early age, I had distorted images of myself etched on to the canvas of my mind. I grew up in an era before "Black was Beautiful," and "Dark was Lovely." As a dark-skinned girl, I was called every variation of "black" imaginable. It was not a term of endearment or meant to be complimentary, but derogatory and demeaning. Even in the African American community, a good majority were conditioned to believe that only fair-skinned girls with light eyes and long hair were pretty. My first encounters with discrimination came from within my race, not from without.

My mother did all she could to shield me from the taunting and what might be called "bullying" today. She did everything in her power to boost my ego and build my confidence. Unlike most dark-skinned girls who were told growing up that they should only wear dark colors like navy, brown, and black, my mother always dressed me in beautiful, bright colors. I wore yellow, orange, sky blue, and all the colors of the rainbow because she said those colors brought out my skin tones. In her attempt to give me a sense of worth, she told me black goes with everything. I called my mother the night of the 2014 Academy Awards when Lupita Nygon'o won an Oscar wearing a beautiful light blue dress. This further validated her training was right, and she did not mind letting me know!

My mother also armed me with quips and retorts I could use as a defense mechanism against the harsh words said to me. "Sticks and stones may break my bones but names will never hurt me," was a popular saying I recall shouting often. Kids can be cruel and in reality, the names did hurt. I did not know it then, but later learned just how powerful those words were and the affect they had on me.

Insert those childhood experiences with society's views and it was almost impossible for me to live through that period of my life and come out emotionally unscathed. Negative images of blacks were pervasive. The contributions and accomplishment of blacks were absent from my history books, and positive role models in the media were rare. I still remember the embarrassment I felt when studying my fifth grade American history book and the only images that looked like me were slaves. At eleven years old, I wanted to slide under the desk. I could not escape the insecurities, scars, and distorted perspective I had of my own worth and value.

WHO AM I?

All of us transition from adolescence into adulthood with some kind of (real or perceived) baggage that we must work through. Images from television and magazines create feelings of not being pretty enough, good enough, smart enough, tall enough, or thin enough. It may be your complexion, your size, the shape of your nose or eyes, your weight or height that you do not like about yourself. Suffering from low self-esteem and flawed self perceptions based on someone else's biased portrayal of what the standard should be is common, and I was no different.

One evening during my search for my identity, I was home alone and having an internal battle as I struggled with an announcement I recently made to my family members. I was leaving the fellowship where all of my church-going family attended. I was breaking ranks and joining Full Gospel Church in Greensburg, a multi-racial, non-denominational church 45 minutes away.

My mother and my aunts made up the family council of sorts and they asked questions: "Why are you going there?" "Who do you know there?" "Are you sure that is what you want to do?" My mind was made up and I had no doubt it was the right move for me and the right time. I shared with them the two dreams I had where I was temporarily separating from my family. There was nothing negative said, but I knew my decision did not set well and was not met with overwhelming enthusiasm.

My family was not the only ones with questions, I had plenty of questions myself. Why am I so different? Why is it I do not fit in? I wondered why I could not be like my mother and her sisters. They seemed to be able to just go along and get along. Why do I hear the beat of different drum? Why am I the one who had to blaze new trails in the family? I had so many questions. I was genuinely seeking answers.

That night I cried so hard and poured out my heart to the Lord for what felt like hours. After I finished my little tantrum and pity-party, the answers came. In my spirit I heard, "You are unique and I made you that way. I did not make you to be like anyone else. You are fearfully and wonderfully made. I made you with your strengths and your weaknesses, gifts, talents, and abilities. I made everything about you just the way I wanted it and I love you. You are made in my image and likeness, accepted by the beloved, and how dare you not accept yourself?"

Love your neighbor as you love yourself.
MARK 12:31, GW

I was totally blown away by the response to my questions. Those words resonated in my heart over and over again. From that point forward, I never thought of myself the same way. Tears flowed as I laid in bed repenting and asking forgiveness for not loving and accepting the person God created me to be. That encounter revealed my true value and forever secured my self-concept. God let me know that He was not a respecter of persons and He loved me unconditionally.

For the first time in my life, I really knew my worth was not tied to the color of my skin, what people said, thought, where I lived, or where I went to church. The amount of money I have or which side of the tracks I grew up on did not determine my value. My self-esteem is solely derived from the fact that I am made in the image and likeness of God. Regardless of my socioeconomic level, job title, weight, color, or marital status, nothing will ever be able to change that. I emerged from that experience an empowered, secure, affirmed, and confident woman.

NO ONE CAN MAKE YOU FEEL INFERIOR WITHOUT YOUR CONSENT

Eleanor Roosevelt said it best, "No one can make you feel inferior without your consent." I have shared with so many people over the years who struggle with their identity. All of us are unique, no two fingerprints are the same, and our eyes are as distinctive as the stars.

I recall reading about Jesus asking His disciples, "Who do men say that I am?" The disciples answered with the opinions of men and every answer was wrong. Men will identify you incorrectly every time. Peter, gave the correct response, but only because it was revealed to him by the Father, not because he relied on flesh and blood (Matthew 16:13-16).

Knowing who you are, accepting who you are, and being content with who you are is an important step to becoming single and satisfied. I was comfortable with myself and the woman God made me to be, but I was still a long way from being content—Single and Satisfied.

ALWAYS THE BRIDESMAID

Wedding bells were ringing all around me, and everyone was getting married, or so it seemed. One by one my best friends were getting married. I was genuinely happy for each of them and shared in their excitement. I bought beautiful dresses, planned bridal showers, bought gifts, and celebrated every union. I even coordinated and sang at their weddings. The more time elapsed, the more my circle of single friends narrowed.

As with most singles, I spent an exorbitant amount of my time consumed with discussing the shortage of good men and wanting to be married and have children. My single girlfriends and I would get together and chat for hours. We would discuss the most recent statistics and current ratios of women to men. We would talk about every article or study that came out about how our chances of marrying were decreasing the more educated and the older we were getting. "Where are all of the good men?" we asked as our biological clocks ticked away.

Priorities, finances, and schedules change with marriage. The biggest change for me when all of my friends married was that I did not have anyone who had as much time or discretionary funds available to do the things I still loved to do. In spite of the negative connotations around being single, there were benefits. I could still travel, make my own decisions, and set my own schedule.

There were so many things I wanted to do, but I did not have anyone to do them with. I was alone and lonely. Work, home, church. This was my weekly routine and I was ready for a change.

"I've learned by now to be quite content whatever my circumstances."
PHILLIPIANS 4:11 (MESSAGE)

LIVING SINGLE

One day, the words "occupy until he comes" resonated within me. I knew the phrase was in the parable of the ten talents, but it was saying something totally different to me. To me, those words meant get busy, do something, live, until "HE" comes. The "he" could be husband or the "He" could be Jesus, regardless, it was time for me to live life.

It was at that point when I decided to live a fulfilled, complete life and maximize the moment. The days of being a "single merely existing" or a "single in waiting" were over. I was going to enjoy living single.

Venturing out to Full Gospel Church was a transition with multiple purposes. I did not know what to expect, but I was excited and anxious about being in a new environment. My first service I arrived early, ready for a new experience. Service started on time and the people were warm and friendly. The music was different, and clapping on the one and three count instead of the two and four count would take some adjusting. Overall, it was a great atmosphere for worship.

I attended the early service most of the time, but one particular Sunday, I attended the 11 a.m. service. Afterwards, I saw a couple young ladies I had never seen before and we introduced ourselves. They were Khristie and Niecy Dennis. They were friendly, outgoing, and single. We began to hang out and forged friendships with other singles in the church. We went to conferences, watched movies, and traveled together. We were living single and enjoying it. Meeting Khristie and Niecy that Sunday was a divine connection.

SERVING WITH GLADNESS

"The unmarried woman careth for the things of the Lord."
1 CORINTHIANS 7:34

The next fourteen years were phenomenal. The connection to these two women eventually led to me being one of the first eight members of The Lord's Church, founded by their father, Archie L. Dennis, Jr. Niecy and I became best friends. The Lord's Church grew and I fellowshipped with many wonderful people. I established many lifelong relationships that I still cherish to this day. I grew and matured into a content, single and satisfied woman.

My fulfillment came as I served faithfully in ministry. I worked at the Lord's Church untiringly. If the doors were open, you would likely find me there. Over the years I worked in several ministries and was able to cultivate my gifts. I led worship, headed up the administration team, worked in the office, worked in finance, and conducted training sessions and workshops. I was a member of the Pastoral Advisory Board, strategic planning committee, and the Board of Trustees. I helped coordinate seminars, conventions, and retreats.

Pastor Dennis was known and respected around the world and I think he knew everyone. As part of the inner circle, I was given once in a lifetime opportunities to meet and interact with some of the greatest voices in Christiandom.

As hard as I worked in ministry, I played just as hard. I have always loved to travel and I worked to saved money for the next trip. I vacationed in Puerto Rico, Aruba, the Caribbean, and went on several cruises. Every year, I took a trip to New York to see a Broadway production. I took a bus trip to Toronto to see plays. My girlfriends would get together for an adult sleepover to catch up with each other's lives and to solve the world's problems as we talked and drank coffee all night. I was living single, and in my estimation living large.

In addition to working hard in ministry and playing hard, I also prayed hard. Prayer was as much a part of my normal routine as anything else. My friends and I would meet some Friday nights to pray. We shared our concerns with each other and we were each other's prayer partners. As a single, it was time to work on developing my personal relationship with the Lord. I attended conferences and workshops, and I went to hear various speakers. I loved God and I loved my life.

Valentine's Day is typically a single person's worst "unofficial" holiday. I knew I had arrived to a place of contentment when I no longer had a need or desire to attend the annual Single's Valentine's Day party. I had passed the test. I was comfortable going out to dinner and sitting alone on Valentine's Day. I was also comfortable sending myself flowers: "To me - From me - With Love," if I felt so inclined.

I mastered going to see a movie alone, without an entourage and without one moment of feeling subconscious. There was not much more that I desired to do as a single woman that I had not done. I was satisfied—single and satisfied.

Chapter Two

It's A New Season

I felt I had reached the pinnacle of living a single, satisfied lifestyle. I had learned to be content. If I never married, I knew I was a complete, well-rounded, and whole person. I often said, "The man who marries me is going to have to catch me!" I was not going to let any grass grow under my feet sitting around, pining my life away waiting for someone to fulfill or complete me.

Through the years I had matured spiritually, naturally, and emotionally. I had a great job, completed two degrees, traveled where and when I wanted, and I was sitting on top of my world. I teasingly told myself and others that I would marry a doctor or earn a doctorate by age 50. One evening, it occurred to me that there was no one looking into my big brown eyes, so it was about time for me to start working toward that Ph.D.

Organizational dynamics always intrigued me and Regent University's Organizational Leadership program piqued my interest. I wanted a degree that I could use in either the faith-based or secular arena and Regent's distance learning program topped my list.

The first thing I did was count the cost. Both of my degrees were paid for by corporate reimbursement programs. Westinghouse paid for my undergraduate degree in Business Management and Mellon Bank paid for my Master's degree in Training and Development. I was paying for this degree and tuition for a Ph.D. was expensive. I remember thinking as much as I would be paying for this Ph.D, they should give it to me. Nonetheless, I disciplined my spending, paid off all my bills, started living off half my salary, and I saved the rest.

1999

To everything there is a season, and a time to every purpose under the heaven: a time to plant, and a time to pluck up that which is planted …
—ECCLESIASTES 3:1-2

The world was abuzz with predictions about what the year 2000 would bring. On a global scale, the dawning of a new millennium was on everyone's mind. 1999 was a pivotal year. Prince, the Artist, produced an entire album called 1999. He wrote a popular song, that epitomized the moment: "Cause they say two thousand zero zero, party over, oops out of time. So tonight I'm gonna party like it's 1999." No one really knew what was going to happen, but all eyes were on the year 2000.

On a personal level, I shared the same feelings. I knew change was eminent. I was ready for the new. Veteran's day was Thursday, November 11 and working at a bank, I had the day off. I felt the need to spend some quiet time in prayer and meditation and asked permission to go inside the church. I had a key and I was sure it would not be a problem.

I went in about 9 a.m. and a friend joined me. I prayed for any number of people; family, friends, my pastor, the church, and eventually for personal direction. As I was meditating, in my spirit I heard the words, "Prepare your bags for moving." I sensed that meant I would soon be leaving The Lord's Church, I just had no idea when. I shared this with my friend and continued to ponder it in my heart.

November ended with a visit to Regent University for a Preview Weekend. The decision to go back to school was a major one and I needed to know more details about the doctorate program. I was making a four to seven year commitment and was well acquainted with the sacrifices required. My social life and time with friends and family would quickly disappear and be replaced with reading assignments, research, studying, and writing papers. I left Virginia Beach, excited, focused, and I was "looking2BPHD."

SEASONS CHANGE

I first heard Israel Houghton sing "It's a New Season" in the fall of 1998. A friend had attended a worship symposium at Cornerstone Church in Toledo and brought me a copy of the conference.

The song was recorded "Live" and CDs were ready the following year. I received my *first* copy in the fall of 1999. I say first copy because everyone loved the CD. I purchased several copies that I kept giving away.

I distinctly remember receiving another copy of the "New Season" CD on December third. That was the evening I went to a meeting at Zion Christian Church. I had never attended the church before (and have never attended again after) and I had no idea what was in store for me that night. The meeting was in a recreation room and we were seated at tables. There were only 15 – 20 women present. Sharon Potter was the speaker and immediately after worship, she was drawn to me like a magnet. I did not know her or anything about her and I was a little guarded. It did not take long before I was convinced she was the real deal.

She accurately spoke to me about things I had expressed to God in prayer. I was speechless as tears streamed down my face. Then she told me of a new season I was about to enter into during the year 2000, a season of great persecution and false accusations. If that wasn't enough, she saw people making me big promises that would not be kept, a "too good to be true" deal that was a trap, and many misunderstandings. Thankfully, she also spoke of God keeping His promises to me, a new boldness, humility, new opportunities, and ultimately, it would be all worth it when God vindicated me. She concluded by releasing an anointing for fulfillment and I have never seen or heard of her since.

I was totally blown away. My thoughts were racing at the speed of light as I sat there in tears, trying to process what I had just heard.

WHAT COULD BE WORSE?

For days I thought about the words I received from a total stranger. In my mind, I relived the horrible time when I suffered through the loss of my grandfather in 1989, my grandmother in 1990, and my oldest brother in 1992. It was the saddest period of time for me and my family. I was emotionally depleted and more acquainted with grief than I ever wanted to be. In spite of the despair, I continued to give God thanks through it all.

That Sunday I stood in the pulpit leading worship with Bill Gaither's song, "Because He Lives." My cheeks were wet with tears as I sang the chorus:

Because He lives, I can face tomorrow,
Because He lives, all fear is gone
Because I know He holds the future
And life is worth the living
Just because He lives!

"And life is worth the living, just because He lives!" became my personal reality and more than just a song.

ACQUAINTED WITH GRIEF

Living through the deaths of multiple loved ones in such a short time was one of the hardest things for me to get through.

I was just 23 years old when my father died and my grandfather had become the father figure in my life. He meant the world to me, I adored him. He was my biggest supporter and there was nothing I ever needed that he did not give me. He was so proud that I was working and going to college.

He was the patriarch of the family and when he spoke EVERYBODY listened. He was a strong, hardworking man who reverenced God, loved his wife, and his family, always putting their needs before his own. He was an excellent example of Christ loving the church. I wanted to see my grandfather's face when I showed him my college degree. I had dreams of him walking me down the aisle when I got married. I had so much love and respect for him. His death devastated me.

My Grandmother lived around the corner from us when we were growing up. I am the only daughter of a daughter and I always felt I was the benefactor of the traditions, values, and teachings my grandmother instilled in my mother. The first day of school, Easter, Christmas, and any special occasions, I always had to go over to Grandma's for her inspection and approval. She was the personification of a lady—such a wise woman. She made clothes without a pattern, she canned peaches, made preserves, and crafted beautiful quilts. She was a true Proverbs 31 virtuous woman.

The "widowhood effect" is a term used to describe the death of a grieving spouse shortly after the death of their mate. My grandparents were happily married for over 60 years and my grandmother never stopped grieving. When she died, many of our family traditions died with her. Her death paralyzed my mother and her sisters and for the first time, I had to get involved and participate in planning a funeral. Talking to undertakers and going to pick out a casket were things I shunned like a plague. I was the one who avoided everything and anything related to death. I did not want to talk about death or think about it, but now I had to grow up.

Even more difficult for me was the loss of my oldest brother, my "Bubby." I grieved his death the hardest. He was seven years older than me and always protective of his little sister. He baby sat me and made the best fudge and French fries in the world. Our childhood was too short. He went off to college and then to Viet Nam.

Like so many others blessed to return home, when he returned from the war he was never again the same. We lost him to a life of drug addiction. We prayed intensely for him and God answered our prayers. He gave his heart to the Lord and his conversion was as miraculous as Saul into Paul. His nature changed from a fearless lion into a gentle lamb, a big teddy bear. The brother I grew up with was restored. *"And I will restore to you the years that the locust hath eaten, the cankerworm, and the caterpillar, and the palmerworm…"* (Joel 2:25). God restored all of our breached relationships tarnished during those years and it did not take Him years to rebuild them. I had my big brother again and I wasn't ready to let him go so soon.

Less than 90 days prior to his death, I had visited him in the hospital and led him to the Lord. We went to church together and had dinner together as a family every Sunday during that time. Our "Prodigal" was home and we threw him a big party. We killed the fattest calf, bought him a new suit and a new pair of shoes. He knew the story and asked, "Where is my ring? You forgot the ring."

There was no "elder brother envy" with us. We were glad to have our brother back home. He and I were closer than ever before. My family would sit around for hours and talk, laugh, and reminisce about our childhood. We joked about stories that no one could really understand or appreciate but us. We listened intently to his stories about the numerous times his life was spared, some of the crazy things he did, and of the amazing grace God extended to him.

Now, he was gone again. Yes, he was with the Lord. Yes, he was in a much better place, and yes, he was not in the streets anymore … and I was grateful. None of that eased the pain in my heart; it still hurt badly to lose my brother.

"Lord," I wept, "What about his children, his babies?" His youngest son was only two years old and his youngest daughter was five. My heart ached every time I would look into their little faces and see my brother. I prayed for strength. "Oh God, help me," I cried. Three of the men

I loved the most were gone: my father, my grandfather, and now my brother.

I thought about Sharon Potter's warning words and asked myself, "What could be worse?"

Y2K—THE NEW MILLENNIUM

The arrival of the new Millennium was uneventful. Computers worked and businesses continued to operate. I was in high gear and purposefully preparing for school. All of my energy was focused on the doctorate program. On March 6, I received my acceptance letter and classes started in August.

Going back to school meant I had to change jobs and the timing couldn't have been better. I loved my job, but working long hours and the rigorous schedule I kept would be impossible once I started school. On a regular basis I traveled to Los Angeles, Dallas, Atlanta, Chicago, and Boston. I enjoyed the travel, but I sensed changes occurring in our organization that did not align with the direction I was headed. My job search led me to an opportunity to be an independent consultant with a pharmaceutical marketing firm. The pay was higher and the schedule allowed me time to pursue my education.

In March I was assigned a special project. I had to find a company who could consult and implement ISO 9000 in our division. I had done extensive comparisons, research and interviews, and finally narrowed my search down to the final three consultants. I planned for this to be my last major assignment and I wanted it to be excellent. Our executive team consisted of a team of well-educated men, including a Harvard graduate. I attended to every detail to make sure there were no surprises.

I informed my contacts of the composition of the team and asked them to send their best. In walked Mr. Michael Batchelor.

Michael was articulate, knowledgeable, and masterfully handled the meeting. I took a backseat and strategically positioned myself around the table so I could see the reactions of the executive team. I asked one question that I already knew the answer to so those present could hear the expert's response. I knew how much more receptive executives are when a consultant says the same thing you said. Later two of my male colleagues and I took Michael to lunch and afterwards he was headed back to Detroit.

The conversation over lunch was business, baseball, current affairs, and some meaningless bantering comparing Pittsburgh and Detroit. As we were leaving the restaurant Michael gave me a polite comment and said goodbye. I went back to work to finish out the day not expecting to hear from or see Michael again. End of story … or so I thought.

Michael called a few times to follow up on the status of the consultant job. Initially, I was totally oblivious of his subtle expressions of interest. Once I became aware, I was short, curt, and all about business. He was persistent, but eventually got the message and stopped calling. Late one afternoon (at his boss's direction according to him), he called to see if they were still in the running for the contract. I gave him an update and decided to tell him I was leaving the bank and who he should contact in the future. That was the conversation that broke the ice. He gave me three numbers and asked that I call him if I was ever in the area. I told him it was not my practice to call men I don't know and I would not be calling him. Before I left Mellon Bank he had my cell phone number.

Every Memorial Day weekend, my church hosted an annual Believer's Convention and I invited Michael to attend. He came to Pittsburgh with his best friend and met all of my friends and a few family members. He went with me to the private reception my pastors hosted after service. I had numerous responsibilities during the convention and thank God my friends had my back because I was a little pre-occupied.

There is the pursuer and the pursued, the hunter and the hunted. He made it clear that weekend, he was in pursuit. Wedding bells were in my future.

EVERYTHING MUST CHANGE

Any change, even a change for the better, is always
accompanied by drawbacks and discomforts.
—ARNOLD BENNETT

I was still moving forward preparing for school. My finances were in order, I had purchased the books for the first semester, and I was ready to go. There was a requirement to be on campus for two weeks in August and I had my time off approved. I was feeling anxious and overwhelmed as the first day of school rapidly approached. I decided to call Dr. Winston, dean of the School of Business and Leadership. I wanted to ask his advice about attending school this semester with the fury of activity I had going on in my life.

Dr. Winston and I had spent some time talking at the Preview Weekend I attended in November and he remembered me when I called. We talked for almost 20 minutes. I told him all that was going on in my life, how hectic things were getting with planning a wedding and preparing to move to Ohio. At the end of the conversation, he recommended I put off starting until my life settled down. I had to send a letter of my intentions. I spent months rearranging my life so I could attend school and now the reality of not going was sinking in. Was I doing the right thing? Was I just delaying or totally giving up my dream?

I wrote the letter to Dr. Winston and stared at the screen for what felt like hours. I could not bring myself to push send. I sat there, not moving, frozen like a mummy and suddenly, the email disappeared. It was gone. Sent. I could not believe it because as God is my witness, I did not move. I sat there and cried as my dream to earn a Ph.D. went up in smoke.

When You Least Expect It

Through the years, I always said I would marry out of The Lord's Church. I always believed my husband would come from outside the TLC circle. I never thought I would marry there and remain a member forever.

Michael and I were getting married. I had a new job and traveled Monday through Friday. My church involvement was scaled way back from the days of being at church every day for two or three weeks at a time. I was only home on weekends now, limiting my church activities. I was out of the loop and out of touch with the behind the scenes activities and conversations taking place.

Marriage

I always desired someone who was more intelligent than I thought I was and who had a more diverse life experience than I did. I was raised in church and lived a relatively sheltered life. Michael was a brilliant man—the smartest man I had ever met. He had his Juris Doctorate, graduated number one in his class, and he had a mind like a computer. He knew everything (or so he thought) and he loved to talk. He had a sense of humor, second only to his mother, and he would have you laughing for hours telling one story after another.

Michael also had a past that included the broader life experiences I wanted. He was no different than anyone else. To my knowledge, Jesus was the only one who ever lived a perfect life on this earth. Romans 3:23 says, "For everyone has sinned; we all fall short of God's glorious standard." I had certainly made plenty of my own mistakes along the way and so had those who sought to be judgmental and critical. I believed the same God that forgave me of my past wrongs, forgave him of his and that was the end of the story. He was the desire of my heart, the man I asked God for and I loved him.

DISAGREE WITHOUT BEING DISAGREEABLE

Everyone was not in agreement with my choice. Just three weeks before my wedding my best friend told me she could not stand with me as my maid of honor. I was stunned and hurt. I cried all night long, then collected myself, chose my matron of honor, and proceeded to move forward with my wedding plans.

I learned several sayings and lessons during my fourteen years working closely with Pastor Dennis. One of my favorites was, "You can disagree without being disagreeable." Niecy and I agreed to disagree. Our friendship changed, but our relationship did not end. She is and always will be my sister.

From all of this I learned a great lesson. Relationships change with each transition and one of the consequences of my season change was my relationship with my friend. As perfect as our relationship was in the current season, it would be a disaster in the new season I was embarking upon. Bittersweet as it was, it was necessary.

Pastor Dennis taught us to disagree without being disagreeable by both precept and example. I personally witnessed him maintaining relationships with people in spite of the fact that he was not in agreement with them. In my fourteen years working closely with him, I do not know of anyone he insulted, ignored, or wrote off because he disagreed with them.

Pastor Dennis and I also had several candid discussions prior to my leaving. Though we never saw eye-to-eye or shared the same opinion on events that occurred or my upcoming marriage, we spoke our truth in love and at the end of it all, we agreed to disagree.

Why the situation played out the way it did was not known to me at that time. It became clear to me one year later. Feelings were hurt on both sides and we were both disappointed, but we remained respectful and handled ourselves with dignity and honor.

LEAVE RIGHT

Over the years I witnessed so many members leave the church angry and upset because of a disagreement, their choice of mate, or a misunderstanding. In spite of the fact I did not like how things were handled, I determined in my heart to be an example of how to leave right. I did not spew my personal feeling about the situation all over the church. I was not seeking allies nor was I looking to be a victim. I only wanted to do the right thing before God and walk out what I believed He was directing me to do. Only my closest family and friends knew specific details or heard about the deep hurt I felt.

Pastor Dennis and I talked about my last Sunday there and how my leaving would be handled. It was undeniable: I had served God, my pastor, and The Lord's Church faithfully. Upon that fact, we were in 100% agreement.

I wanted my pastor's blessing because in his words, "I came in the front door and I was leaving out of the front door."

SWEET SORROW

For us to ever get to a new level or a new tomorrow, something has to end. Dr. Henry Cloud wrote a book called, *Necessary Endings,* and as bittersweet as endings are, they are necessary. Every new beginning starts with an ending. Endings are the prerequisites for any new beginning.

Sunday, October 8, was my last service at The Lord's Church. Feeling anxious, I woke up early and dressed for church. Countless times I've scurried out to my car on my way to Haymaker Road in Monroeville. I had driven those back roads hundreds of times and I knew them like the back of my hand. I had a 40 minute drive and I became the queen of putting my eyeliner on at the red lights.

EVERY NEW BEGINNING STARTS WITH AN ENDING

I was alone with my thoughts and they raced through my mind like a locomotive. So much had happened over the last few months that I was just ready for the day to be over. My emotions were all over the place. I was glad it was my last Sunday, but I was sad at the same time. I was not just leaving my church, but also my friends, memories, history, and cherished relationships. I was leaving everything I knew and loved to embark upon a new adventure—marriage.

I cherished every minute of the service, every song, and every word. At the end of the service, Pastor Dennis and the faithful elders called me to the front of the church, and gathered around me to pray God's blessing over me as I went my way. As I stood in front of the church with my eyes closed, hands raised, tears rolled down my face and I heard the sniffles from the congregation. I opened my eyes and I was surprised to see so many in tears and wiping their eyes. If a stranger would have walked in they would have thought it was a funeral.

We cried so much, it was hard. There is nothing like having a church family who supports you and genuinely loves and cares for you. We had been together for so long, shared so many awesome memories, and I was grateful for my time there. After the prayer, Pastor Dennis had words and presented me with a framed Certificate of Appreciation for fourteen years of faithful service. An hour after service, we were still at church loving on each other, embracing, and saying goodbye.

Later that year Pastor Dennis had a 65th birthday celebration that we did not attend. Two and half months had passed and I still needed time to myself and more time to recover, and do some healing. I needed some space and time to process my leaving. I later sent him a birthday card and a monetary gift. He sent me a thank you card and a copy of his book, The Garbage Man's Son. He autographed the book and wrote, "You will always be my daughter." I cherish those words, the card, and his book. For some odd reason, I even kept the copy of the canceled check with his signature.

Michael and I attended the Believers Convention that May. Seven months had passed since I was gone and it was great to be home. The service was well attended and it was a large crowd. I saw Pastor Dennis on the platform and he did not seem like his normal self to me. I had not seen him in a while and I thought he might be fatigued. After service he was surrounded on the platform by his guests and well-wishers. My only regret is that I did not push through the crowd to greet him that night. It would be the last time I would see him alive. Five months later on Friday, October 26, I received a disturbing call that Pastor Dennis went home to be with the Lord. I was stunned, frozen in my tracks at the sad news. What happened? Shocked and in total disbelief, I could not believe what I had just heard. My husband held me as I cried. Late into the night, my phone rang as The Lord's Church members, family members, and friends called to make sure I had heard the news.

"Oh God," I prayed, "the family … the church." I was a part of them and I had to be there with them. The next morning I packed and headed to Pittsburgh. A two and half hour drive in a car alone is a long time to reflect. There was one consoling thought, we were on excellent terms. I had no guilt or remorse, only the pain of loss to process.

Never in my wildest imagination would I ever have thought that in less than thirteen months after leaving The Lord's Church, I would be getting dressed to attend the Homegoing service of my former pastor. I arrived early and the church was full as I expected. Pastor Dennis treated the person who carried his bags with the same dignity and respect as he did any of the Gospel greats who were quickly filing in the church. Pastor Dennis was well loved, a peacemaker, and a bridge builder. Former members from the start of the church lined the balcony to pay their respect. I knew so many of the distinguished attendees from my interactions with them over the years that the current staff asked me to handle the special guest seating section. It was my privilege to serve Pastor Dennis and The Lord's Church one last time.

THE ASSIGNMENT

I gave my heart and soul to The Lord's Church. I had a vested interest in its success, skin in the game; I worked untiringly to help bring the vision to fruition. My labor could not be in vain. All of those words spoken over the house ... I grieved as if I had lost a loved one. I spent time in intercessory prayer for the family and the church members. I reminisced about the excitement of the early days, the splendor, and the anointed pageantry. I had no rest and no peace until the day in prayer the Holy Spirit whispered and assured me, "The glory of the latter house would be greater than the former." Those words gave me peace. Now, I could finally release the old and move totally in to the future.

I now fully understood that my assignment was to play an integral role in the inception of The Lord's Church but did not include the transition.

"We know that God makes all things work together for the good of those who love Him and are chosen to be a part of His plan."
—ROMANS 8:28, NLV

Chapter Three

HAPPILY EVER AFTER

My life would never be the same. The year 2000 saw me move away from home and my family for the first time in my life. I changed my marital status along with my lifestyle, cities, states, residence, jobs, and churches. My world as I knew it changed forever.

Everyone imagines having a long, enduring, and happy marriage. On any given day, couples stand at the altar dreaming of sharing a lifetime full of love, joy, and laughter together. Your average person does not intentionally enter into marriage planning for anything less than living happily ever after. We promise to stay together through the ups and downs, through thick and thin, in good times and bad. For better or worse, for richer or for poorer, in sickness and in health, to love and to cherish until death do us part … While we say those words and believe our love will survive it all, we pray for and fully expect "better, richer, health." No one ever prays for or anticipates "worse, poorer, or sickness."

OFFENDED BUT NOT OFFENSIVE

Michael was not in agreement with how I handled my transition and departure from The Lord's Church. He felt I should have just left the church and never looked back. He was offended because of the way things transpired. My history would not allow me to handle myself in that manner. I have never left a church because I was mad, angry, or offended and I had no intentions of starting.

Leaving, for me, would have been the easy way out. It was harder to stay through altercations, love through the hurt feelings, and cry through the disappointment. I denied myself and I crucified my flesh because somewhere I was taught that was what Christians were required to do.

I believed when God directs you to attend a church, He already knows every situation you will encounter: the good, the bad, and the ugly. He knows who will be kind to you and who will be like sand paper, rubbing you the wrong way. He also knows every misunderstanding, inequity, disagreement, and awkward moment you might experience even with leadership. Jesus told his disciples it is impossible that no offenses would come (Luke 17:1).

People get offended. In the course of lifetime, "coming and going" is a part of church life, but the repeated "goings" to avoid conflict only stunt spiritual growth. One thing Pastor Dennis always said, "You take you with you everywhere you go." Changing churches doesn't change you. The names and faces may change, but you will run into the same situation you left until you pass the test. I've also seen those who were offended and did not leave. They stayed and criticized, murmured and complained, but never passed the test. Either course of action impedes spiritual growth and delays your ability to receive the full inheritance of blessings and prosperity promised in the Word of God.

Clean Hands

The LORD has rewarded me according to my righteousness,
according to the cleanness of my hands in his sight.
—Psalm 18:24 NIV

Being offended is a choice, but it was not my choice. Some were jealous of my relationship with my pastor and used the occasion of my departure to say disparaging remarks about me. There were a few who stopped speaking to me, gave me the cold shoulder, and chose to miss my last service because they were not in agreement with my choices and my decisions.

My husband and I agreed on our perspective of what occurred, but we had vastly different opinions on how to handle it. I made a decision to stay through the challenges and pray through the difficulties. He did not understand at first, he felt I had a greater allegiance to my pastor, my church, and my friend than I did to him. I had to help him understand that my first allegiance was to God and to pleasing Him.

I shared with Michael that from the time I was a child, my mother taught me that I was not responsible for what people did to me or said about me. I was only responsible for my response to what they did or said. She taught me God would hold me accountable for my reaction, not the actions of others. She told me God was always on the side of right and if I did what was right, God would work it out, validate, and vindicate me.

There have been many times in my life that I have wished those words were not etched indelibly on the table of my heart. Right isn't always easy. My first inclination, like anyone else, is to do unto others worse than they have done unto me. I knew how to act as unseemly as the next person. You hit me, I will hit you back harder. You hurt me, and I will hurt you even more. Time and again, I cried because I wanted to lash out, strike back, and defend myself, but my mother's godly teaching and the Holy Spirit constrained me. I was taught to pray and give it to the Lord and let him judge the matter. It was engrained in my spiritual DNA.

Michael had been a criminal defense attorney— a master at making his case and arguing his points. He learned that this was just one argument he was not going to win. There were many other voices in my ear with varying opinions of what they would do or what I should do. At the end of the day, I would stand alone before God and be judged for my actions and my motives. I held to my convictions and I did the right thing. I had a proper ending and I was ready for a new beginning, a fresh start.

CHURCH SEARCH

One of the first things we wanted to do after getting settled in to our new life was find a church home. I prayed for God's direction and guidance as we searched for a church that would meet our spiritual needs and where we could enjoy worshipping together. There were a few Sundays we would get up, get dressed and head out to an eleven o'clock service at random. We would sit in the service taking in the worship and the sermon.

Afterwards, we would always talk about our first impressions, share our observations and how we felt about the service. On a couple occasions, we knew in the first 20 to 30 minutes we were in the wrong place. We would give each other that certain look and quietly excuse ourselves and go to breakfast. It is sad to say but there were some Sundays I felt my time would have been better spent watching wrestling ... and I am not fan of wrestling. Have you had something in your mind that you could not describe, but you knew it when you saw it? Nothing else measures up. We knew what we wanted and we would recognize it when we found it.

I continued to pray for guidance and direction as our search stretched past two months. It was now the last week of the year. We had just spent our first Christmas together and we both had time off from work for a few days. Early one morning around 6:00 a.m. my husband woke me up out of a deep sleep to show me a young couple preaching together on television. It was the first time either of us had seen a husband and wife team preaching together before and that immediately caught our attention. We were blessed by the broadcast and hoped they were a local ministry. They were. We scrambled to find a pen and paper to write down the address and we decided right there we would visit the church that Sunday.

NEW YEAR—NEW SPIRIT

It was the last day of the year, Sunday, December 31 and we headed to the 8:30 a.m. service. Michael printed the directions and we discovered the church was 45 minutes away. Still new to the area, we did not know the east side from the west side, had we known, we would have likely continued to look for a church a little closer.

We could not have chosen a worse day to visit the church. Everything that could go wrong went wrong that morning. The weather was awful, one of those horrible Cleveland storms. The roads were icy and unplowed, visibility was low, and it seemed like we were driving to the other side of the world. We were sliding all over the road and that 45 minute drive took us over an hour. We thought of turning around and going back home but we persevered.

New Spirit Revival Center was led by Pastors Darrell and Belinda Scott. Our first service was awesome—the worship was great and the word was excellent— we both knew we had found our new church home. The church was huge and a totally different culture from the small, family-oriented church I was accustomed to attending. We called the pastors the dynamic duo. We loved the fact that they preached together and both of them were powerful speakers.

I had already decided that I was not disclosing anything to anyone about my background or previous church involvement. It had been a very long time since I just sat in the congregation, enjoyed the service, and went home. I wanted to worship with Michael by my side. It was a time of refreshing for me and I savored the moment. Our travel schedule did not allow us a lot of free time to get involved with any of the weekly services or activities, but we attended as many special events as we could. We participated on clean up days and tagged along with the Nursing Home ministry on occasion.

COLLISION OF HISTORIES

Dr. Myles Munroe said, "Marriage is a collision of two histories, not the coming together of two people." He was visiting my church shortly after Michael and I were married and I was moved when he shared that marriage was not two personalities, but two histories that come together and then a lifetime of discoveries. As I sat there and did the math I thought, "There are 98 years of history colliding here," … and collide it did.

I was a very strong, independent woman when I married. I was cautioned often as a single woman, "You may want to tone down or 'dumb down' a little because a man might find you intimidating." According to the dictionary, to "dumb down" is to reduce the intellectual or developmental level, and I was *not* about to do that. I was not needy or desperate and I was not about to tone down or dumb down anything to get a man. My response was always, "The man that is intimidated by me is not the man for me." I happened to believe that a strong woman just needed a stronger man.

So you can just imagine the adjustment dilemma marriage presented for me. One of the best things that helped me was that we both traveled during the week. Michael would leave out Sunday evening and return Friday evening and I would leave Monday morning and return home Friday morning. I thought it was a marriage made in heaven, the best of both worlds, and a blessing from the Lord. I laughed as I told my friends, "God smiled on me because He knew I needed to be eased into marriage one weekend at a time." Our histories collided for short periods at a time on Saturday and Sunday.

Your Gift Will Make Room

I heard about Women's Educational Mentoring Alliance, a women's mentoring and leadership training course that was starting and I thought it would a good opportunity to meet and establish a rapport with some of the ladies in our new church home. When I picked up an application, I knew my days of sitting in the pews were numbered. The application asked for prior ministry experience and required a pastoral letter of recommendation.

I completed my application and included a short list of the ministries and responsibilities I was involved in at my previous church. Before his death, I had also received an excellent letter of recommendation from Pastor Dennis that I included. Shortly after my application was submitted, we were asked to meet with Pastor Darrell and begin attending leadership meetings.

9/11 CHANGED EVERYTHING

Tuesday, September 11, 2001 changed everything. A typical work day, I had an early flight from Colorado Springs to Dallas, Texas. I was all strapped in on the plane and attendants were preparing for takeoff. I was on the phone with Michael and the doors were shutting. I told him I would call him when I landed and I loved him. I said a prayer as is my custom and I settled in ready for departure.

During the flight while talking with the flight attendant the pilot announced we were going to be landing in Amarillo, Texas. I asked, "Did I just hear him say Amarillo, Texas?"

"Yes," she answered, "I am going to see what is going on."

I sat there for a moment wondering if I had taken the wrong flight. The pilot did not give us any more information until after we landed. He told us there had been an incident unlike anything that had ever happened In the United States before. He instructed us to take all of our things. By this time everyone's cell phones were ringing and we were getting bits and pieces of information, but I was still not aware of what happened —our nation had been attacked by terrorists and all flights had been diverted to the nearest airport.

My phone rang as soon as I turned it on and the first thing I heard was Michael saying, "Quita, get off that plane!" I could hear both panic and relief in his voice. I told him, "The doors aren't open yet, what's going on?" He wouldn't tell me any details until I was off the plane and safely in the terminal.

I headed to the rental car counters and I could not get a rental car without a reservation. I was more concerned about where I would stay and my travel agent booked me a nearby hotel. I spent the rest of the day glued to CNN, on the phone, full of anxiety, my heart racing, and tears flowing. All I wanted was to go home to my husband and to be closer to my family.

The following day, my travel agent was able to get me a car and I drove to my next meeting in Dallas. I drove from Amarillo to Dallas, facilitated my meeting with the doctors and after a few hour sleep, I drove from Dallas to St Louis, and then on to Cleveland. Over 1,500 miles I drove across country. I had a view and perspective of our great nation that most only saw on television. People were friendly and American flags were proudly raised everywhere. All of the planes were still on the ground leaving hotels virtually empty except for those of us fortunate enough to have obtained a rental car. The stress and apprehensions of that ordeal caused me to have heart palpitations for months afterwards.

9/11 permanently changed everything about air travel. A little over a month later Michael and I had a Caribbean cruise planned for our first wedding anniversary. It was my first time returning to an airport since 9/11 and the heightened maximum level of security was still in place. I felt like I was in Beirut or some other foreign country as I watched soldiers with what looked to me like these humongous M16 rifles walking around the airport. I had never been that close to a real gun before and it shocked me into a reality that I struggled to wrap my mind around. As much as I loved to travel, the necessity of a military presence as a norm was a cause to pause and take note.

Once on the plane, my flying routine did not change. I always pray for traveling mercies and protection. We had a great anniversary celebration and returned home safely. On the cruise, we decided that week to look for employment that did not require as much travel, we wanted to get more connected to the church, and we decided to set up our own business. In May of 2002, MARMIK Training & Consulting was incorporated.

Starting our own business endeavor allowed us to spend more time together and become much more active in church. We were faithful to attending church every Tuesday, Thursday, and Sunday.

A man's gift makes room for him and sets him before great men (Proverbs 18:16). It was not long until we were asked to be involved in several ministries. I was on the finance team and placed over the New Members Ministry. I taught leadership classes and became an instructor and board member of the Women's Educational Mentoring Alliance. Michael worked with the pastor on the church's business affairs and he also taught Shepherd's and New Member's classes.

THE DECISION

One hot Tuesday evening in the summer of 2003, we were having a pot luck fellowship at church and Michael and I were asked to go take a look at a house. We had no idea where it was located and I had no idea why we were looking at it. I was content with our current residence and I was not interested in moving, but it was something to do and I thought, "There's no harm in looking." After a 25 minute ride, we arrived at a home in a quiet, upscale suburb.

We were given a full tour inside and outside. There were three floors of all the things you would love to have in a home. Fire places, a hot tub, jacuzzi, master suite, sun room, wood floors, chandeliers … the works. We went back to church and chatted about how lovely the home was and I thought that was the extent of the conversation. We had a wonderful evening socializing with those we knew and meeting others who were new to the church.

Somewhere during the course of the evening, without my knowledge or any discussion with me, Michael had a conversation and communicated we liked the house and would take it. "You told him what?" I shouted. "How dare you make a major decision like that without my input or agreement?" This was a major collision of our histories of epic proportions. I was livid, and in no uncertain terms I was pretty vocal about making my feelings known.

DECISION MAKING

I am a practical person and pragmatic in my decision-making. I had so many questions and there were no answers. How much would it cost, how much would be needed for a down payment, what condition was the house in, were any repairs needed? Had I known we would be the next tenants, I certainly would have looked with a different eye.

I like to think about, talk about, and pray about decisions—especially major ones. I treasure relationships and I've never been one to intertwine business and personal relationships. I have passed up an opportunity to buy a condominium next door to my best friend because our lifestyles, personalities, and views on privacy were different. I valued our friendship and did not want to jeopardize the relationship.

I'm sure Michael's heart was in the right place and he meant well, but had we discussed the move, I would have weighed all of the pros and cons, counted up the cost financially, and argued long and strong about the risk of doing business with church leaders. My response would have been, "Thank you, but no thank you."

Regardless of my disagreement, Michael was not going to back out on his word. At the end of the day I did what wives do, I acquiesced and went along to get along. We signed an agreement to rent with an option to buy, deposited thousands of dollars, and in September we moved from the West side to the East side.

It has been said that if it seems to be too good to be true, it usually is. The move was unexpected and unplanned and I was uncomfortable with it. The house was huge and without the beautiful living room and dining room furniture that was included, it would have been empty and our voices would have echoed in the corridors. Michael and I were grateful and appreciative. I was hopeful things would work out.

By the end of 2003, Michael and I were living in a new house, serving the Lord with gladness, and life was good. We were both ordained as elders in November of 2004.

Chapter Four

For Richer or Poorer

"The blessing of the Lord, it maketh rich, and he addeth no sorrow with it."
—Proverbs 10:22

Charles Dickens wrote in the opening sentence of *A Tale of Two Cities*, "It was the best of times, it is the worst of times ..." Life with Michael was certainly the best of times, but the loss and grief coming would, without a doubt, categorize the next few years as the worst of times for me also.

Personal Recession

I grew up hearing my parents and grandparents talk about how they survived the Great Depression. I never dreamed that I would experience my own personal financial depression.

For most of my life, I had a decent job, made good money, and was fiscally responsible. I was raised to pay my tithes and to pay my bills. I met my financial obligations and in my family, I was the lender and not the borrower. That is not to say I have never been buried in debt before, but it was through no fault of my own. There were times when I found myself left holding the bag, but no matter what, I always had enough to maintain my existence.

I handled the finances in our marriage. My husband had no problem coming home, giving me the money to budget and do as I saw fit. Seemingly out of nowhere, our money got funny and our finances became tighter and tighter. I was freelancing and no longer had the steady income from pharmaceutical marketing. Michael had several assignments postponed or cancelled. That, coupled with a large house payment, and it was not long before we were living off credit cards and sliding deeper and deeper in debt.

We both aggressively submitted proposals for work and contracts and I started looking for employment. Michael had his juris doctorate and I had a master's degree, but even with several advanced degrees between us, nothing opened up for us. There were a couple of occasions when I was a final candidate only to receive a call that an internal candidate had suddenly surfaced. I had a Human Resource Representative who felt so bad about the eleventh hour candidate cropping up, ask if she could forward my resume on to another company she knew was hiring. I realized that this was no accident and I knew doors were closing for a reason. I was convinced that unless God opened a door for me, it was not going to happen, regardless of my education or experience.

> *"But remember the LORD your God, for it is he*
> *who gives you the ability to produce wealth."*
> —DEUTERONOMY 8:18 NIV

Church Administrator

I continued to pursue a course back to pharmaceutical marketing which meant 100% travel. Michael had been spending some time volunteering at the church office, and he mentioned there may be an opportunity for me to work there. I had worked in a church office before and I clearly understood the dynamics—financially, personality, and organizationally. We needed income and any salary was better than no salary at the time. What I did not know was that I was walking into a hornet's nest filled with jealousy, pettiness, sabotage, and backstabbing. Another layer of testing was being added.

Our Great Depression

"We are troubled on every side, yet not distressed;
we are perplexed, but not in despair."
—2 Corinthians 4:8

Robbing Peter to pay Paul quickly became a thing of the past because Peter had nothing left to give. Everything was behind: bill collectors calling and shut off notices were the norm. Things were so bad that the gas was turned off for lack of payment one summer. We used an electric plate to cook and to boil water to bathe. I wrapped coins to buy food or gasoline.

I did not have a lot growing up as a child, but my parents insulated us from any of their financial worries. I had no point of reference for this level of financial despair. It wasn't 1929 or 1939, but it felt like it to me.

I was having my own personal, great depression. Someone once said, "Necessity is the mother of invention," and out of necessity I learned quickly how to navigate through these rough and turbulent waters.

SUFFERING IN SILENCE

Suffering in private is not nearly as bad as suffering publically. We owed money on the house and it was obvious that we were being whispered about with some among the church. I was snubbed and ignored as if I were invisible. There were those who literally stopped speaking to me as if I had done something personally to them. Some passed judgment and gloated over the situation. So many days I read and prayed, Psalm 35:19: "Do not let those gloat over me who are my enemies without cause; do not let those who hate me without reason maliciously wink the eye."

During this season, my integrity and personal ethics were challenged. I was questioned about money, falsely accused, lied on and lied to. My character was assassinated by people who demonstrated they had little of their own. Figuratively speaking, I had stab marks in my back from the backstabbers, backbiters, and haters who thought I was unaware of their words and their actions.

Yet, in my obedience to God and my desire to please Him, I did not say a word in my own defense. It appeared that all that was being said about me was true. I often hear people say, "I don't have to take this," or "I don't have to take that," but there are some things you <u>do</u> have to take if you are going to be a disciple of Christ. Jesus did not have to take beatings, being spit on, the crown of thorns or the cross, but he did. He could have called thousands of angels and avoided dying on the cross, but He surrendered to the will of God. Jesus did not answer His accusers and I could not answer mine. Christlikeness was being required of me, and tearfully I denied myself and died on my cross.

The words to the old spiritual became my mantra: "Victory, victory shall be mine. If I hold my peace and let the Lord fight my battles, victory, victory shall be mine."

Every area of my life was in a state of upheaval. On top of everything else I was dealing with, Michael was not feeling well and we had no idea what was wrong. Despite my consistent pleas for him to go see about himself, he refused. He dismissed his symptoms as heartburn or indigestion but his breathing became more and more labored. We also noticed his steps were slower and he was making fewer and fewer trips downstairs. I began taking his meals upstairs as his movement was more restricted and he became more confined. His health grew worse and I grew more concerned.

Still, I faithfully put on my church face and wore my church smile and continued on as if everything was alright. I suffered in silence like so many often do. I was thankful to get through one day at a time. "In Him I live, I move and have my being" was more than a scripture to me. It was my reality. My daily prayers were:

Give me this day my daily bread.
As my day is so shall my strength be.
One day at a time sweet Jesus that is all I'm asking of You.

BREAKING THE SILENCE

There were several very low points during this season, but one stands out more than others. I remember leaving church one afternoon and I called my mother to ask her for money to pay our house payment. It was a day I will never forget. Never in my life had I ever had to call my mother and ask her for money to keep a roof over my head. Worse yet, I did not ask for a loan or to borrow money, I asked her if she could give me the money because I knew I had no means of paying her back.

As soon as I hung up the phone I burst into tears and cried uncontrollably. I have always been independent. I have never liked to ask anyone for anything, but my prideful, independent spirit was being crushed and it hurt me deeply. I cried until I started to hyperventilate and I had a migraine headache. It was in that moment I heard the Lord deep in my spirit whisper to me, "My grace is sufficient." I continued to weep as I found great comfort in those words. I would need those words to carry me through what lie ahead.

THE STORMS OF LIFE

Storms are a part of life and everyone has them. Storms come in all forms. Your storm may be physical, financial, marital, political, or emotional, but as sure as you live, one day you will have some kind of unexpected storm suddenly arise in your life. It does not mean God does not love you or that you have done anything wrong. It means you are alive. You will still have critics and judges like Job's friends who want to ascribe the reason you are in your storm. I certainly had gossipers and whisperers that were vocal about their opinion of my storms, until they were confronted with storms of their own.

One of the first Tuesday night prayer meetings I attended after discovering New Spirit Revival Center, I distinctly remember being on my knees praying, weeping, and telling God I wanted to know Him better. There was a discontentment in me and I wanted more. There had to be something deeper to my Christian experience and I wanted it. I wanted to know Him, not *about* Him … I wanted to know *Him.* I prayed a portion of Philippians 3:10, "That I may know Him, and the power of his resurrection."

I assure you I stopped short of quoting "and the fellowship of His sufferings, being made conformable unto His death" part of the scripture. God was answering my prayer and I was in the middle of the storm. I wanted the power of the resurrection, but there is no resurrection without a burial and burial is preceded by a death. It did not matter whether I prayed it or not. I had enough Bible knowledge to know there are some storms you can speak the Word to and others you must ride out.

SPEAK TO THE STORMS

I did not study meteorology, but I do know there are different types of storms. In Luke 8:22, Jesus' disciples were being obedient to His instruction to go to the other side of the lake and a storm rose up. They were doing the will of God and He was on the boat with them, but that did not keep the storm away. They found themselves in the middle of a life-threatening situation.

When Jesus told the storm to stop, it stopped. His disciples said, "Who is this? We do not know Him like this." (My translation for "What manner of man is this?") He showed them a facet of Himself that they had not seen before.

I had read about Jehovah Jireh, the Lord my provider for years. I sang, "Jehovah Jireh, my provider, His grace is sufficient for me, for me, for me." I sat in church for years and heard sermons about "the Lord will make a way out of no way." I heard them say, "He may not come when you want Him but He's right on time." Really? Really? "God, where are You now at a time when I need You most," I cried.

He was there with me just like He was with the disciples, and ready to reveal Himself to me in my storm of lack as Jehovah Jireh, the Lord who provides. He was there in my storm of confusion and chaos to reveal Himself to me as Jehovah Shalom, the Lord my peace. He was right there.

RIDING THROUGH THE STORMS

A "go through" storm will not respond the same as a "speak to" storm. I stood on the Word and I quoted Philippians 4:19, "My God shall supply all my need according to His riches in glory in Christ Jesus." I quoted David in Psalm 37:25 over and over again, "I once was young and I now I am old, but I have never seen the righteous forsaken." I decreed and declared, "Lord, I am the righteous of God in Christ and I am also the seed of the righteous," yet, my situation remained the same. I was in a Tsunami and I had to ride it out.

> *"And the rest, some on boards, and some on broken pieces of the*
> *ship. And so it came to pass, that they escaped all safe to land."*
> —ACTS 27:44

Eventually I understood I was in an advanced, accelerated "Processing, Refining, Perfecting" class. I was being stripped, broken, humbled, and refined in the furnace of affliction. I was getting my Ph.D., but not the one I started in Organizational Leadership from Regent University. I was getting a Ph.D. in how God can faithfully bring you through Pain, Heartache, and Despair.

I grew up hearing Bible stories about Daniel's deliverance out of the den of lions, Abraham's test of faith, and Joseph's pit and prison experiences. But now it was my turn to live my testimony. In a court of law to be a credible witness you must present firsthand knowledge of the facts. Hearsay evidence is not admissible because it is provided by someone who is relating what they heard and not what they know themselves.

God revealed himself to Daniel, Abraham, and Joseph and now He was revealing Himself to me. He was revealing to me that He was the same God and He had not changed. He was demonstrating to me that He was able to deliver me out of my den of adversity, raise me up out of a financial pit, release me from people's prison, and mature my faith.

It took me awhile to figure out that the season of testing I was in was not about the lack of money, the snares, glares or mistreatment by people—it was about God revealing Himself to me as the only true and living God. Every test was pre-ordained, pre-approved, and custom made to authenticate my testimony and make me a credible witness with firsthand evidence of His faithfulness.

> *"… and ye shall be witnesses unto me both in Jerusalem, and in all Judaea, and in Samaria, and unto the uttermost part of the earth."*
> —ACTS 1:8

There were many dark days and nights when I felt alone and abandoned. I prayed and cried out to God for help but there was no relief. It seemed as if the heavens went silent on me. Everything I ever thought I knew about God, everything I was taught, everything I had ever read was challenged. "God, are you real?" I asked in my despair. My faith in God was shaken to the core and I cried out, "My God, why have You forsaken me?"

HANDFULS OF PURPOSE

*"And let fall also some of the handfuls of purpose for her, and
leave them, that she may glean them, and rebuke her not."*
—RUTH 2:16

Why I never signed up for government assistance, I do not know,
our income would have certainly qualified. I did sign up with all of
the temporary employment agencies in the area. They all said I was
overqualified for the type of assignments they offered, but that did not
matter to me. When they called me, I went and worked whatever project
I was given. I remember going to one appointment and for whatever
reason after a couple hours, they sent me home. I later received a check
in the mail for $16.00 after taxes. I can laugh about that now but it was
not funny at the time.

In the book of Ruth, Boaz instructed his men to leave Ruth handfuls
of purpose as she gleaned in the fields. Gleaning in the fields was God's
welfare system for providing for the poor. During this financial crisis in
my life, I learned God as Jehovah Jireh, He was my provider. I was not
on welfare, but I was on Godfare. I talked to God and He would talk
to others.

HERE A LITTLE AND THERE A LITTLE

We had family who provided financial support when they could, and
I had faithful friends. Three specific occasions stand out in mind. I
received a call from a friend in Pittsburgh and she asked me, "How

are you guys living?" It dawned on her Michael was sick and could not work and I did not have a job. I told her we were struggling, but making it. She told me she had just received a bonus and was going to send me something. She said she could not have money sitting in a bank knowing she had a friend in distress. I never said anything to her about how bleak my financial situation had become, but God did.

On another occasion, I was ironing something to wear to the hospital. I had a shut off notice from the electric company and I did not have the money to pay. Michael would be home in a few days and I did not want him worried about the bill or coming home to no electricity. At the very time I was thinking and praying to God, the buzzer rang and it was Federal Express. I was surprised because I knew I had not ordered anything and I was not expecting a package. I opened the package and another one of my friends had sent me a check for $500.00. It was more than enough to pay the electric bill and again God was teaching me He was my provider. If I talked to Him, He would talk to someone on my behalf.

I recall being in church with only having $3.00 to my name. I decided there was nothing much I could do with $3.00 so I put it in the offering. Before service was over, one of the elders asked me not to leave before I saw her. I was at the door when she caught me and gave me a $50.00 bill.

I had other friends who were praying for me and would call often with a word of encouragement. True friends are revealed in hard times and in times of crisis. I was grateful to God that I had no surprises in that regard. My friends were there for me and stood by me. I am equally grateful to the "frenemies" and "famemies" (friends and family) who identified themselves to me too. It was helpful to have an advance copy of the guest list with the names of those who would be in attendance when God prepared the table before me (Psalm 23:5).

NARROW PLACES

God is not Santa Claus nor is He a magic genie. There were numerous times when He did not answer my prayer or send someone to meet a need. God was looking for me to have total dependency on Him. This journey I was on was my personal lesson in faith and trust in God. I realized how personal it was one night as I read and meditated on the Twenty-Third Psalm.

David said, "Even though I *(not we)* walk through the darkest valley, I *(not we)* will fear no evil because You are with me *(not us)*." This path was so narrow, there was no room for anyone else but me and God. God was the only one who could bring me through the worst days of my life. My mother, my brother, my pastors could not do it, only God. God deserves all of the glory and all of the praise. No human being, dead or alive, can take any credit for my deliverance. Only God gets the glory!

I said all that to say this: when you look around and the people you think should be there for you are not, do not get angry with them. First of all, unless you are a minor child, no one is required to do anything for you. Secondly, it just could be God has the place you are in so narrow and so tight, there is no room for anyone but you and Him.

"The LORD had said to Abram, 'Leave your native country, your relatives, and your father's family, and go to the land that I will show you.'"
—GENESIS 12:1, NLT

In order for Abram to become Abraham and the Father of Faith, he had to get out away from his family. He had to get away from the familiar and away from those who would act as crutches. God's ways are so much higher than ours and I could see why I had to marry and move away. Silly me, I thought it all about the love.

I have a very close knit family who believes in rallying to help family members in distress, and my mother is usually the one who leads the efforts. If we were living in Pittsburgh, my family would have never allowed me to go through the financial devastation or suffer the great losses that I did.

My mother offered to move us to Pittsburgh, put us in an apartment, and pay our living expenses until Michael was healthy or I had a job. I could have taken the easy way out but had I done that, I would not have known God like I know Him today or matured in my faith. I would not have the testimony of God's faithfulness or of Him making me an overcoming, conquering, and victorious Christian.

"And lo, I am with you always, even unto the end of the world."
—MATTHEW 28:20

Chapter Five

FOR BETTER OR WORSE

*"For the thing which I greatly feared is come upon me,
and that which I was afraid of is come unto me."*
—JOB 3:25

The stress of the financial situation had taken an emotional and physical toll on both Michael and me. As our financial woes intensified, so did the tension in our marriage. Money problems can ruin a marriage and is one of the leading causes of divorce. In our frustration, we worried, panicked, and argued. Add to that Michael's anguish over unfulfilled promises that left him disenchanted, disillusioned, and disappointed. Michael was made promises from those he trusted that did not pan out. I did my best to caution him and to help manage his expectations. His encounter with the humanness of people he held in high esteem caused him much angst and shook his confidence in man, ministry, and God. I was his sounding board as he vented and expressed his dismay and I encouraged him to keep his eyes on Jesus, the only one who would never fail him.

The strain of it all overwhelmed us. I gained weight, suffered hair and memory loss, and experienced heart palpitations. The pressure was so unbearable at times, I thought I would lose my mind. I laid hands on my own head and prayed Isaiah 26:3 (NLV):

> *"You will keep the man in perfect peace whose mind*
> *is kept on You, because he trusts in You."*

Through it all I prayed, cried, and praised God through every setback and set up. I felt like the widow woman in the parable with the unjust judge. I would wake up saying, "It's me again, Lord." I was continually casting my cares on the Lord. I thank God I was able to sleep at night. Sleep has always been my altered state of consciousness. I did not have vices to help me escape reality, so I took naps. I determined if I ever woke up in the middle of the night, it was to pray. Many nights my pillow was wet with tears and I travailed in prayer seeking God's help and deliverance.

My husband on the other hand, would be up all through the night. He also prayed, but internalized his feelings. Men like to fix things and he could not fix our financial condition. He carried the heavy burden of all that we were going through as well as many other unresolved issues of his own. All of this turmoil showed itself in Michael's physical body as he continued to weaken. I begged him to see a doctor but medical attention was still out of the question. We did not know it at the time but he had a heart attack (which I will talk more about in the next chapter).

HERE COMES THE DREAMER

I was praying and praising and believing God, but it was out of a place of fear and not faith. I was praying about what was going on around me, what I could see with my eyes. I was praying by sight and not by faith until I had a dream.

I have always been a dreamer. So much a dreamer that some of my friends nicknamed me Josephine. In March of 2005, I had a dream where I saw myself standing on top of a very high mountain. As I stood on the mountain, I was holding an American flag in my hands and tears were streaming down my face. It was a dark and dreary day and grey clouds were all around me. I noticed the flag was unlike any I had ever seen before. It was very dirty, tattered, war-torn, and the length of it was about one fourth of a flag's normal size. As I was standing there with tears running down my face, I planted the flag on top of the mountain.

Suddenly, the scene changed, the sun began to shine brighter than I had ever seen it shine before. The dark, grey clouds were now beautiful, puffy white, and the sky was a vivid bright blue. The flag changed too, right before my eyes, and right in my hands. The flag turned into a brand new, full-size, red, white, and blue American flag with all of the stars and stripes. In an instant the ragged flag was transformed and blowing in the wind as I stood there rejoicing and praising God.

I meditated on the dream for several days and pondered its meaning for weeks. I remembered the image of American soldiers in World War II raising the flag at Iwo Jima and I knew the dream symbolized a hard fought battle, a fierce fight, and a major victory.

The American flag is sometimes referred to as "Old Glory," and I summed it all up to mean it's time to give God glory because this season was coming to an end. Clearly, the dream was God-given and it was a sign of a turning point. Nothing changed about my situation, but I changed in the situation. With this prophetic dream in my spirit, something changed inside of me. Faith was ignited in my heart.

My prayers changed from, "Lord, deliver me," to "Lord, I thank You for the victory, I praise You for making me more than a conqueror." I had a spiritual vision of victory and I was holding on to it for dear life. I possessed it and I embraced it even though nothing around me had changed for the better. As a matter of fact, the worst was yet to come.

THE MOVE

"The rich ruleth over the poor, and the borrower is servant to the lender."
—PROVERBS 22:7

We were a few months in arrears and we received a final notice to evacuate the house. Michael handled all communications regarding the house including delinquent payments. He acknowledged that their patience exceeded what could have been expected. I had no idea where we would live or where we would get the money to move but God was proving to me over and over again His faithfulness and that He was with me. We found a place with no trouble and our families gave us the money to move.

Michael was too sick to help move anything. I had to pack up everything and move out of the house into an apartment by myself. Several times a day I packed boxes, loaded the SUV, drove 45 minutes, unpacked, and went back again. It was hot and humid. I was humiliated, embarrassed, tired, disappointed, hurt, and angry. I never wanted to move in the first place and thousands upon thousands of dollars were wasted.

Right or wrong, I was not a happy camper and anyone who knew me heard about it. Many times during this horrible ordeal, the words

I received from a stranger in 1999 haunted me. "In the next season … I see something coming along that is going to look like a really good deal. It's going to be too good to believe and, the Lord says, 'It is.' It's just a trap …"

LIGHT AT THE END OF THE TUNNEL

We were at last totally moved into our new apartment. I was sitting out on the deck relaxing and reading my Bible. As I sat there, a little bird landed on the railing. I sat watching the bird, and the spirit of God began to speak to me about how He takes care of the little sparrow and He would take care of me. He spoke to me about the lilies of the field and how they don't toil, but they are clothed and beautifully arrayed. He reminded me that the hairs on my head were numbered and He was with me. In my distress, God met me and ministered to me. All I could do was sit there and shed more tears.

This long chapter of financial despair was finally easing. Pastor Darrell always says, "When a test has accomplished its purpose, it will end." There were many lessons learned during this season. God took me from walking in fear to walking by faith, from worry to worship, from complaining to confidence, and from questioning why to simply trusting Him.

"He brought me up also out of a horrible pit, out of the miry clay, and set my feet upon a rock, and established my goings."
—PSALM 40:2

Chapter Six

In Sickness and In Health

I tried unsuccessfully for months to persuade Michael to see a doctor. His health gravely concerned me and I prayed daily that he would see about himself. He was visibly sick and his breathing was increasingly more labored. Michael could only walk a few steps without tiring, so it was a good thing we were out of that big house and everything was on one floor.

August 17 Michael finally decided to see a physician. An EKG revealed that he had suffered two heart attacks. The doctor wanted him hospitalized immediately and was ready to call an ambulance. He told Michael 50% of the people who had heart attacks like the ones he did, died instantly. This explained the reasons for Michael's shortness of breath, fatigue, and inability to walk more than a few steps at a time. Once again, God showed Himself to be merciful and faithful.

Even though Michael had been ailing for quite some time, we were in total shock and could not believe what we were hearing. We tried to pinpoint when the heart attack actually happened, but that proved impossible. We recounted an episode when he woke up sweating profusely and another time when he thought he had a bad case of indigestion. We were not sure when or where the heart attacks occurred, but the evidence was indisputable.

The doctor called Admissions to make arrangements for Michael and there were no beds available at the time. Michael convinced the doctor to allow us to go to lunch while a bed was being cleared before we went to the hospital. Once we arrived, Michael was admitted with no delays. Test results showed his heart was pumping at a low rate and he needed a quadruple by-pass. Because Michael had neglected his health so long, his body was in no condition to safely undergo the operation. He spent nine days in the hospital in preparation for the surgery. I was there with him every day.

The surgery was scheduled to take place on a Tuesday. Michael was released the Friday before so he could have a little break from the hospital before undergoing the procedure. He was feeling and looking better and we took a day trip to Detroit. His parents were older, unable to travel, and they were anxious to see their son. Everyone had been so worried about Michael's health that all the family came over to see him. It was a very emotional visit. He later told me he did not know whether he would survive the surgery and he was saying his final goodbyes.

We enjoyed our time together. We talked, laughed, and had a wonderful weekend. The evening before surgery, I decided to check the job sites one last time to see if there were any new positions posted since I last checked. There was a position listed and when I read it I thought, "This was written just for me." I applied for the job and then called it a night. We had a big day ahead.

I remember the day my husband had quadruple by-pass surgery the way most Americans remember the day Hurricane Katrina devastated

New Orleans. The after effects of Katrina were working their way across the states with heavy rains and power outages. I remember praying that the power would not go out while Michael was on the operating table. The surgery took several hours and I was at the hospital alone the whole time. Many thoughts raced through my mind and I experienced many emotions as I waited. I was concerned about Michael coming through the surgery and I was concerned about taking care of him by myself when he came home. The sight of blood made me queasy, and I had never cared for anyone with incisions or changed bandages.

Happy Anniversary

There were people praying for Michael across the country. I asked everyone I knew to pray and God answered our prayers. Michael's surgery was a success! His heart function improved and eventually exceeded the expectations of his cardiologist. He was feeling better than he had in years and we were optimistic about picking up the shattered pieces of our lives. We believed things were turning around for us and we were thankful.

In October, we celebrated our fourth wedding anniversary at the Ritz Carlton courtesy of special friends. After the difficult year we had been through, this anniversary was more meaningful than any of the others. It was extra special and we enjoyed every moment of it. We reaffirmed our love and privately renewed our vows to each other. For the first time in a long time, Michael was hopeful and spoke in positive terms about our future. We celebrated our love, his new lease on life, and my new job.

There was another reason Michael thought this anniversary was special and it had nothing to do with me or anything romantic. Our hotel room was on the Concierge level and several of the Philadelphia 76ers basketball team stayed on the same floor. Michael had an opportunity to meet the head coaches and he listened in as they talked about upcoming game strategy. Michael loved sports and this made his day. Our fourth wedding anniversary was memorable … a five-star celebration that I will never forget.

Unfortunately, our celebration was short-lived. Before the end of October, Michael had a setback in his progress. He complained of leg pains and shortness of breath. His ability to walk and climb stairs was impaired again, just like before his open heart surgery. This was upsetting and felt like Déjà vu. "After all he has been through, this just isn't happening again," I thought. What in the world could this be? We soon found out. Michael's condition worsened as his lungs filled with fluids, pleural effusions. This was quite disconcerting for both of us and quickly dampened Michael's spirit.

Frequent office visits and numerous procedures followed, but nothing seemed to help. I knew something was seriously wrong on Thanksgiving. From the time we married, it was our custom to spend Thanksgiving holiday in Detroit with Michael's family. Thanksgiving dinner at my mother-in-law's was a longstanding Batchelor family tradition and we always looked forward to it. Michael wasn't feeling too well but managed to get through the holiday. He promised his mother he would see the doctor the following week and he did. The doctor wanted Michael back in the hospital, but he refused to go. It was the holiday season and instead he elected to have an outpatient procedure that brought him temporary relief until after Christmas.

Christmas was Michael's favorite holiday and in spite of all the ups and downs, we celebrated this one with grateful hearts (literally and figuratively). Michael had a long list of items he wanted for Christmas.

Among them was a particular photo printer. I determined to find it and I was frustrated going from store to store looking; but, this Christmas, Michael would get everything on his list.

By God's grace, we had survived another tumultuous year. As we embarked upon a new year, Michael expressed his feelings in a poem he entitled, *"Arise New Sun."*

ARISE NEW SUN

NEW YEAR, NEW START
NEW PLACE, NEW HEART
NEW DREAMS, NEW LIFE
NO STRESS, NO STRIFE
MOVE ON, DON'T TURN
USE WHAT YOU LEARNED
MY GOD, YOU SEE
HAS PROMISED ME
HIS LOVE IS TRUE
IN OLD AND NEW
THAT LIFE IS MINE
THROUGHOUT TOUGH TIMES
AND THAT HE'S THERE
AND THAT HE CARES
YOUR TIME ARRIVED
2005
YOUR JOB IS DONE
ARISE NEW SUN
GOD BLESS MY DAYS
AND ALL ITS WAYS
MY HEAD IS CLEAR

IN THIS NEW YEAR
NO TIME TO WASTE
I HAVE NEW FAITH
NEW LIFE STARTS NOW
MY HEAD I BOW
TO THANK THE LORD
FOR HIS REWARD
THAT I CAN STAND
AND SAY "I CAN"
KNOWING FROM ABOVE
THAT I AM LOVED

IF IT'S NOT ONE THING, IT'S ANOTHER

The first week in January Michael was back in the hospital. His condition was chronic and the process of removing fluid from his lungs continued. Over the next few months, he continued to suffer, in constant pain. He experienced stroke-like symptoms and was rushed by ambulance to the hospital. Even though he had no facial weakness or change in speech, this was disheartening. Michael had a few decent days during the first six months where he was mobile and able to work on a limited basis. He was depressed and the death of one of his childhood friends only made him feel worse. The more his health failed, the more withdrawn he became.

In July, Michael became more symptomatic and went to see his primary physician who diagnosed him with pneumonia. After the treatment regimen, there was still little improvement in his overall well-being. He was weak and barely ate anything. These issues persisted way beyond what I was comfortable with and I wanted Michael to change doctors or get a second opinion. It took him months to even see any doctor and he had a good rapport with this one and did not want to switch. Watching him suffer was agony for me. I did my best to take care of him, but I felt helpless. Mind altering medication affects the behavior of those with extended illnesses. There were times I felt like Michael resented the fact that I was healthy and he was sick. People who are sick or infirmed sometimes lash out at the person closest to them, the one they need the most. In reality, they are angry about the situation they find themselves in and the fact that they are in need. They too feel helpless.

I don't know all the reasons for the change in his moods or behavior. I just knew, as with everything else, I was to do the right thing regardless. I did what I could do—pray. My husband was deathly ill and I was afraid for him. I walked in from work every day not knowing what to expect.

Breaking Point

Early in August we made a trip to Detroit to celebrate Pop's (Michael's father) birthday. We arrived at their home and as soon as Michael greeted them, he went straight to the bedroom and lay down. Our visit was cut short because Michael was so ill. On our drive home, he called for a doctor's appointment and his regular primary care physician was not available. On August 7, Michael saw the doctor filling in for his primary care physician. Without hesitation he was referred to a pulmonary specialist. The situation was urgent and Dr. Williams saw Michael August 10. This was an answer to my prayers for a new doctor and a second opinion.

Dr. Williams and Michael hit it off instantaneously. She did her residency in Detroit and that was their common bond. Dr. Williams examined Michael and personally supervised his procedure from start to finish. Unlike the others who repeatedly performed the same procedure, Dr. Williams sent the fluid removed from his lungs to the lab for tests.

Michael was finally ready to go to the hospital. Almost one year to the day of his heart surgery, Michael asked Dr. Williams to make arrangements for him to be admitted to the hospital. He was so weak he could barely stand and we took over two hours to get him up and dressed. He was using a cane and a chair to support himself for a long while. I assisted him from the bedroom to the door but I could not help him down the steps. I called the maintenance workers from our complex and asked them if they could help Michael to the car. He was admitted to the Intensive Care Unit. I stayed with him long after visiting hours were over.

> *For you are my hiding place; you protect me from*
> *trouble. You surround me with songs of victory.*
> —PSALM 32:7, NIV

SONGS IN THE NIGHT

I came home from the hospital and fell on the floor, flat on my face and I cried and cried and prayed and prayed. This was too much for me to bear, I was overwhelmed. I cried so hard I was shaking. As I lay on the floor crying and praying, out of my spirit, I began singing a song that I had not heard or sang since my days of leading worship at The Lord's Church. Morris Chapman wrote the song and the words are:

> *Be Bold, Be strong*
> *For the Lord thy God is with thee*
> *Be Bold, Be strong*
> *For the Lord thy God is with thee*

Do not be afraid, Do not be dismayed
Walk in faith and victory
For the Lord thy God is with thee.

I sang the words to the song over and over and over again. God strengthened me through the song. I continued to sing, pray, and cry. The Holy Spirit pulled out of my spirit another song I had not heard or sung in years. It was a chorus written by Henry M. Davis, my former Minister of Music at The Lord's Church. I sang these words as I lay curled up on the floor in a fetal position.

My God is able, able to do all things
My God is able, able to do all things

My God is faithful, He's faithful to the end
My God is faithful, He'll faithful to the end

My God is worthy, He's worthy to be praised
My God is worthy, He's worthy to be praised

My God is loving, God is love
My God is loving, God is love

My God is precious, more than this world to me
My God is precious, more than this world to me

The words to those two songs ministered life to me and caused faith to arise in my heart. I was once again assured that God was with me. As I progressed through every facet and every phase of my trials, God always brought me songs for strength and comfort. The Bible says, "Faith comes by hearing and hearing by the word of the Lord." Whether the word was in a song or a scripture, it was accompanied by the faith I needed to obtain the victory.

Praise and worship was my place of refuge, my hiding place, my place of solace. I would wake up in the morning, somewhere between consciousness and unconsciousness and I would hear a chorus or one line of a song. One morning I woke up and heard Kathryn Kulhman's voice singing, "Only believe, only believe, all things are possible, if you only believe." I remembered my mother taking me to see her often when I was a little girl. Other songs like, *Come Thou Fount of Every Fountain Blessing* and *On Christ the Solid Rock I Stand* kept me encouraged. All other ground truly was sinking sand …

One night I left the television on overnight. When I woke up I heard the song that would carry me to the end of the journey. I had never heard it before but I remembered enough of it to track it down and buy it. It was Michael W. Smith's song, *Agnus Dei,* it was that song that carried me all of the way through to final victory. I purchased it and played it on repeat; morning, noon, and night. I played it while I slept. I woke up to it and I went to bed with it. It was pure worship, nothing about me, nothing about what I was going through, nothing about help or deliverance. It was all about worshipping God.

THIRTY-SIX DAYS

As I was entering my husband's room the next day, his nurse was leaving. She introduced herself to me and quipped, "I said a little prayer over your husband because he seemed to have given up. I hope you don't mind." I told her I did not mind at all and with those words, I encountered Brandy

McKinney. She was the angel God sent to take care of my husband's medical needs and to help me navigate through the medical maze. At every turn, God had the right someone there for help and support. Brandy was Michael's favorite nurse too. She could get his cooperation and get him to do what none of the other nurses could get him to do. If she was on duty, she was the RN assigned to take care of him.

I was so relieved Michael was at last in the hospital where he could get the medical attention and care he needed. I had done my best, but knew he needed more than I was able to provide. Every day for the next 36 days without fail, I was at the hospital sitting, talking, reading, and of course, praying. There were so many times during his stay that things went awry. I never knew what to expect. On two separate occasions he was over-medicated. I happened to call from work one morning to check on Michael and his speech was slurred. I left work immediately and drove to the hospital to find him unconscious and in a medically induced coma. I screamed as loud as I could for help and doctors and nurses came running from everywhere.

One Sunday, I was getting dressed to attend the 8:30 service before going to the hospital. Before I could leave the house for church, one of the resident doctors on duty called me to tell me Michael's breathing was very irregular and he wanted to put him on a ventilator. I had just been there a few hours ago. I stayed late the night before and he was fine when I left. What happened? Who is this person speaking to me? I didn't know him and he did not have the right answers. I did not give him permission to do anything until I got there. I wanted to talk with one of the nurses on duty who I knew was familiar with Michael's case.

I arrived at the hospital to find my Michael lethargic and unresponsive. Someone put a fentanyl patch on him for pain and he was over-medicated.

He had renal failure and was on dialysis. "Why would anyone put a medicated patch on him?" I asked.

Brandy was there to give him a shot to reverse the effects of the drug and to talk me through the mayhem of what was going on. Michael opened his eyes in seconds and began speaking normally. God was there. By this time, I wanted to move Michael to another hospital, but he did not want to move. I was afraid to leave his side and depending on which registered nurse was on duty, many times, I stayed well into the night.

Michael had an onslaught of physicians: cardiac, renal, cardiac pulmonary, neuro, and a few more. Somewhere around mid-September, I was requested to attend a private conference with all the doctors to discuss Michael's condition. I asked that Brandy sit in the conference with me. I was told my husband was diagnosed with stage IV Hodgkin's Lymphoma and that his prognosis was not good. I sat stunned. The oncologist ruled out aggressive chemotherapy because of renal failure. I did not hear much more after that but they continued to spew out more medical terms that I did not understand. When they left, Brandy interpreted everything for me. I was perplexed as to how Michael could possibly have been under a doctor's care for over a year and by the time he was correctly diagnosed, he had end stage cancer. I wondered if Michael had known but didn't tell me.

Michael had received the news earlier and though I was stunned, I was not rattled. God had so fortified me the night Michael first went to the hospital, I was not moved by what I heard or saw that day. I did not falter in my faith in God. I drew on God's strength so I could be strong for Michael. He needed to draw on my faith and my strength.

Michael did not want many visitors. There were only a few elders from our church that Michael was comfortable allowing to see him. Both of our families lived in other states and I was there alone most days. It was my responsibility to be there, to love, support, and be his advocate. After the meeting with all the doctors, I went into Michael's room and we talked. He was visibly down and I encouraged him to keep the faith and trust God.

It was important that Michael see me as consistent. When I cried, I cried in my car or I cried at home. While I was with Michael, I did not allow anyone—including the doctors—to speak anything negative in his earshot. When they wanted to update me, I would ask that we step into the hall.

I continued to do what I had done every day since the first day he went into the hospital. I read Psalm 91 to him, prayed for him, and sang to him. I am sure I got on his nerves sometimes. I would ask him, "Do you hear me praying for you?" He would shake his head up and down and say, "Yes ... all the time, all the time." For thirty-six days, that was my life.

He who dwells in the secret place of the Most High
Shall abide under the shadow of the Almighty.
I will say of the Lord, "He is my refuge and my fortress;
My God, in Him I will trust."
Surely He shall deliver you from the snare of the fowler
And from the perilous pestilence.
He shall cover you with His feathers,
And under His wings you shall take refuge;
His truth shall be your shield and buckler.
You shall not be afraid of the terror by night,
Nor of the arrow that flies by day,
Nor of the pestilence that walks in darkness,
Nor of the destruction that lays waste at noonday.
A thousand may fall at your side,
And ten thousand at your right hand;
But it shall not come near you.
Only with your eyes shall you look,
And see the reward of the wicked.
Because you have made the Lord, who is my refuge,
Even the Most High, your dwelling place,
No evil shall befall you,
Nor shall any plague come near your dwelling;
For He shall give His angels charge over you,
To keep you in all your ways.
In their hands they shall bear you up,
Lest you dash your foot against a stone.
You shall tread upon the lion and the cobra,
The young lion and the serpent you shall trample underfoot.
"Because he has set his love upon Me, therefore I will deliver him;
I will set him on high, because he has known My name.
He shall call upon Me, and I will answer him;
I will be with him in trouble;
I will deliver him and honor him.
With long life I will satisfy him,
And show him My salvation."

—PSALM 91

Chapter Seven

UNTIL DEATH DO US PART

"The Lord will give strength unto His people; The
Lord will bless his people with peace."
—PSALM 29:11

God gave me the strength to stand through all of the ups and downs during Michael's illness. I stood strong through whatever situations arose. My faith was unwavering and I believed God for healing.

Through all of Michael's illnesses, I was there. I sat by his side, I fed him, I helped him walk, took him to the doctor's appointments, made sure he had his medicine. My face was the last face he saw before they put him to sleep for surgeries and the first face he saw when he woke up. I saw him at his weakest moments and most vulnerable states. Though I held strong, I finally reached a point where I could not bear to see my husband, a born communicator who loved to talk and laugh, unable to communicate at all.

On October 2, Michael took a turn for the worse and I spent the night at the hospital. That had to be the longest night of my life. I stayed in the waiting room because I did not want Michael to hear me crying. I prayed and told God, "This is too much, I cannot take anymore!"

Sitting in the waiting room, I had an unexpected visit from Dr. Williams. By now, I knew the rotation of the attending physician on duty in the Intensive Care Unit and Dr. Williams was not scheduled. Of the four or five attending physicians Michael had caring for him, Dr. Williams was the one we both trusted most. She was knowledgeable, thorough, sensitive, and honest. I could depend on her, no matter the news.

She prefaced the conversation with, "I promised you I would always tell you the truth ..." I felt myself tensing up. She proceeded to give me the shocking news that Michael had only a few days or perhaps only a few hours to live. I don't know how long I stood there, frozen in my tracks, unable to speak. I could not believe what I was hearing. I was overwhelmed with emotions and the floodgates opened. I broke down and sobbed, "I cannot do this any longer, I cannot, I just cannot."

Dr. Williams wrapped her arms around me, held me, and allowed me to cry on her shoulder. Suddenly she began to pray for me. My husband's doctor became my intercessor. She prayed a powerful prayer and though I do not recall all that she said, I will always remember her asking God to strengthen me, to help me, and to guide me when the time would come, to make the hardest decision of my life.

When Dr. Williams came in the waiting room to talk to me, she had papers for me to sign regarding resuscitation. In the state I was in, she recognized I was too fragile emotionally to broach that topic. She left the waiting room never mentioning the papers she held in her hand. That was the last time I ever saw her.

After she left I made phone calls to both of our families and to my church. My mom and brother drove from Pittsburgh to see Michael and to be there with me. I was on edge and anxious that it was taking them so long to get there. I was happy to see them and to have someone with me. After they were with me awhile, I went home to freshen up and change clothes. I was nervous about leaving and I hurried back as quickly as I could. The male elders from my church were outside of the room talking with my brother when I returned.

What Do I Do?

I walked into Michael's room and saw him laying there all wrapped up in what looked to me like a shroud and I totally lost it. I was past my breaking point. I frantically called for the nurses and I insisted that they do something, anything. My mother tried her best to calm me down but to no avail. She tried to explain to me that the nurses were only trying to keep him warm. I had hit my breaking point and I just couldn't handle anymore. For the second time that day I found myself sobbing uncontrollably. Only this time, I was in the arms that held me when I was born. I was once again the little girl, comforted in my mother's arms.

My mother encouraged me, "You have been so strong through everything you've been through, you have to stay strong now."

"I'm tired of being strong. I don't want to be strong anymore!" I sighed.

My tears flowed like a dam had broken and rivers of waters were released. Months of pent up feelings and emotions were unleashed. I trembled as my mother held me.

Eventually I composed myself. My mother and brother headed back to Pittsburgh. Shortly after they left, I was sitting by Michael's bedside when a team of doctors called me in the hallway. They talked to me about my husband's worsening condition and they were looking to me for direction. I stood there staring at them and they stared back at me. I was unable to think. I couldn't move. I could not speak. After a minute or two of silence, I looked at them and asked if I could make a phone call. I left them standing in the middle of the hall and went to call my mother.

"I DON'T KNOW WHAT I SHOULD DO AND THE DOCTORS ARE WAITING FOR ME TO COME BACK."

There was panic in my voice. I said, "Mom, I don't know what I should do and the doctors are waiting for me to come back."

"We are going to turn around and come back to the hospital," she reassured me and as she was speaking, I felt peace come over me. This was a peace that I had only heard and read about, never experienced. It was the peace the Bible speaks of that surpasses all understanding and with that peace came my answer.

In that moment, I heard the words, "It's God's breath and if God wants him to live, he will live." God did not need a machine to keep him alive. "You can go home," I told my mother, "I know what to do."

I hung up the phone and rejoined the doctors still gathered in the hall. I told them the exact words I heard and they told me next steps.

They asked me to sit in the waiting room and told me that someone would let me know when I could return to Michael's room. As I sat there talking with one of the elders, so many thoughts ran through my mind. "What do I say when it happens? What do I do?"

I remembered sometime earlier, a friend gave me Philippians 4:8 to read:

> *"Finally, brethren, whatsoever things are true, whatsoever things are honest, whatsoever things are just, whatsoever things are pure, whatsoever things are lovely, whatsoever things are of good report; if there be any virtue, and if there be any praise, think on these things."*

I returned to Michael's room and leaning on the bed as close as I possibly could, I put my arms around him and began sharing my heart, expressing my love for him, and recounting all of the good times we had together. I started from the day we met and I talked about the joy, the laughter, and the fun times. My face was moist with tears as I thanked him for finding me and choosing me to be his wife. I asked his forgiveness for anything I had done or said to hurt or offend him. I recalled our cruises to the islands, our trips to Niagara Falls, Canada, and Brazil. I asked him if he remembered the time we ate spaghetti for breakfast in San Paulo because it was the only Portuguese word on the menu we recognized—I hope that made him smile.

After I finished speaking to Michael, I whispered a brief prayer to God. I thanked Him for being a Sovereign God. Despite the circumstances, I believed God. If He willed it to be so, Michael would live. "If He does not," I breathed slowly, "I submit to Your will, and I trust Your decision." I sat there quietly alone with Michael, not knowing what else to do or what else to say. In the silence, I heard an inner voice say, "Now, usher him into My presence."

I began to sing praises, glorify God, and worship the Lord. I sang of God's goodness, kindness, and grace. I was so lost in the presence of the Lord that I forgot my surroundings. Time seemed to stand still and the room was engulfed with so much peace. I have no idea how long I worshipped. It was not until I heard the words come out of my mouth, "Michael, I release you," that I was jolted back to reality. Those words startled me and I immediately opened my eyes and looked at Michael— he was gone … Eleven days before our fifth wedding anniversary, I became a widow.

PEACE

Peace I leave with you; My peace I give to you; not as the world gives do
I give to you. Do not let your heart be troubled, nor let it be fearful.
—JOHN 14:27, NASB

The overwhelming sense of peace that came over me when I was on the phone with my mother remained with me over the hours and days that followed Michael's death. God gave me an inner peace that I could not explain. I was not in shock, as some thought, I was at peace. Earlier that day, I was the one being comforted, now, I was the one holding and providing comfort to Michael's nurses as they cried.

All I wanted was to be alone. I sent word to my church by one of the elders who was still at the hospital that I did not want any visitors that night. I had been up over 24 hours and I was physically and emotionally drained. I drove myself home and laid down as I prepared to make phone calls to our families. Looking back on it now, I wanted to linger in the peaceful place I was in for as long as I could.

Whenever I was asked how I was doing, my response was, "I have peace," and I really did. Peace was my barometer as I navigated through funeral arrangements, homegoing services, and all that was entailed in that process. I was determined that my peace was not going to be disturbed. On the one or two instances when it was, I calmly addressed the situation and I returned to peace. I was living the song, "This peace that I have, the world didn't give it to me. The world didn't give it and the world can't take it away."

SAYING GOOD-BYE

There was never any question in my mind about where Michael would be buried. Both of his parents were alive, his family was in Detroit, and I was taking him home to them and the city he loved. I was blessed with wonderful in-laws, Mom and Pops, and I loved them dearly. My heart was broken again seven months after I buried my husband when my father-in-law passed away. Eleven months after Pops died, I lost my mother-in-law. Just as I had sat with their son, I was privileged to sit alone and spend time with each of them before they passed.

On my last visit with my mother-in-law, I talked to her, prayed with her, and told her how much I loved and appreciated her. I did not plan it but out of the clear blue, I began to sing to her. I sang one song after another as a medley of old hymns filled my heart. I started singing:

> *I come to the garden alone. While the dew is still on the roses*
> *And the voice I hear falling on my ear, The Son of God discloses*
> *And He walks with me, and He talks with me.*
> *And He tells me I am His own;*
> *And the joy we share as we tarry there, None other has ever known.*

In my mind I thought, "Where did that old song come up from and how did I remember the words?" The hymns continued to flow and I soon understood, it was a time of ministry and I grasped the moment. The very last song I sang to Mom before I left her was:

> *When peace, like a river, attendeth my way,*
> *When sorrows like sea billows roll;*
> *Whatever my lot, Thou hast taught me to say,*
> *It is well, it is well with my soul.*

Mom could not speak, but I knew it was well with her soul and she was at peace. It was difficult for me to leave her side that evening because I knew it would be the last time I would see her alive. She passed the next morning.

Death parted us all, Michael in 2006, Pops in 2007, and Mom in 2008. For three consecutive years, I returned to the same city, the same funeral home, the same church, the same cemetery ... mourning the loss of those I loved. With each loss, a wound that had not healed was reopened again and again. "Lord, will I ever get over this deep sense of loss, pain, and grief I feel?"

Chapter Eight

AFTER THE STORM

"If we are thrown into the blazing furnace, the God we serve is able to
deliver us from it, and He will deliver us from Your Majesty's hand.
But even if He does not, we want you to know, Your Majesty, that we
will not serve your gods or worship the image of gold you have set up."
—DANIEL 3:17-18 NIV

Until death do us part ... Michael was gone. After he died people asked me if I was angry with God. They knew I was praying, trusting, and believing for his healing. My response was always the same, "No, my faith was in God's ability, my faith was not in the final outcome turning out the way I wanted it to be."

The fury of Hurricane Katrina was short-lived. People weathered the storm and fought to survive, clinging to faith and hope, grateful to be alive. But long after the wind and rain had gone, evidence of the storm's destruction remained. The flood waters receded and the sun came out again, but now it was time to rebuild. The trial didn't end with the storm.

God had given me a song the first day Michael went to the hospital. Now I knew why that song came to me. The words, "My God is able, He's able to do all things," were not just for the beginning of the test but also for after the storm. Faith says, "God is able to do all things whether He does all things or not." Real faith is not tied to a happy ending or a demonstration of God's ability. God is all wise, all knowing and He is sovereign. He does what He wants to do the way He wants to do it and when He wants to do it. Our job is to believe and trust that, "Father knows best."

In Daniel 3:17-18, the three Hebrew boys addressed the King of Babylon in no uncertain terms stating, "Our God whom we serve is able to deliver … But if not, be it known unto thee, O king, that we will not serve thy gods …" Their faith was in the God they served; and, regardless of the outcome, they were going to remain true to their God. Whether my husband lived or died, my faith was not shaken. I believed God was able to heal him up until the moment he took his final breath. Life is not a Hollywood production, and every story will not have a fairy tale ending, but God is able.

> *"And after you have suffered for a little while, the God of all grace, who has called you to his eternal glory in Christ, will himself restore, support, strengthen, and establish you."*
> —1 PETER 5:10, NRSV

WIDOWHOOD

Everyone thought for certain I would move back to Pittsburgh to be closer to my family. The death of a spouse tops the list as one of the most stressful life events. Add to that the strain of a few years dealing with health and financial issues, and it should be easy to see why moving was not on my agenda. I was too fragile emotionally to even consider it. Moving represented another major transition to me and I was not mentally up to the task. I needed time to heal, recover, and be restored.

The first time I heard myself referred to as a widow it sounded like someone was speaking to me in a foreign language. I heard the words, but it took a second to connect to them. Widows are a unique group that are most often ignored. A phrase in Act 6:1 grabbed my attention one day: "... because their widows were neglected." I now understood the neglect of widows in a way that I never had before.

OWE NO MAN

"The rich rules over the poor. The man who uses something that belongs to someone else is ruled by the one who let him use it."
—PROVERBS 22:7, NLV

Cleaning up my credit became an obsession with me. I had thousands of dollars of debt, but I was determined to pay everyone I knew I owed. I started by paying all of the back payments Michael and I owed on the house. Something I know Michael desperately desired before he died.

I also obtained balances from creditors who had written off my credit cards as a bad debt and I paid them off as well.

"A good name is more desirable than great riches …"
—PROVERBS 22:1, NIV

I was told I did not have to pay them, but I did. With me it was a matter of principle and my personal integrity. I borrowed their money, I used it, I owed it, and I paid it. I did not think much of it but based on the reactions I received and the letters of commendation, I suspected this type of thing did not happen often. There is nothing like financial freedom. In time I achieved my goal and I now live debt free.

FORGIVENESS

"For if you forgive others their trespasses, your heavenly
Father will also forgive you, but if you do not forgive others,
neither will your Father forgive your trespasses."
—MATTHEW 6:14-15, NRSV

Mahatma Ghandi once said, "The weak can never forgive. Forgiveness is an attribute of the strong." I thought, "How true." It takes strength to forgive those who intentionally and maliciously do hurtful things to you or say hurtful things about you.

It is human nature to think that you hold the offender captive by holding on to their offense. Nothing is further from the truth. The only person we imprison by not forgiving is ourselves. Forgiveness is a choice, it is not a feeling, and it does sanction the act of the offender. What it does, is free you to move on.

Forgiveness is difficult because it requires you to surrender. When you forgive you surrender your feelings, your ego, your right to be right, your right to get even, and your right to hold the person hostage. It is self-denial, a part of you dies when you release those who have done wrong by you. In Acts 7:60 (NSRV) Stephen was being stoned. It says:

"Then he knelt down and cried out in a loud voice, 'Lord, do not hold this sin against them.' When he had said this, he died."

Stephen was being stoned and "when he said this" ... when he released them, he died. Of course, there was Jesus' example as He was on the cross dying and released His persecutors, His accusers, and His executioners.

I would be lying if I said I did not struggle with forgiveness during the years of testing and trials. It was not easy to pray for those who despitefully used me or to bless those who persecuted me or said evil things. Forgiveness was the final frontier. It was the last hurdle I had to jump over, and the last test I had to pass. It was my path to rebuilding my life after the storm, the ultimate surrendering of my will. Pleasing God meant more to me than harboring feelings of anger, resentment, and unforgiveness. I had too much to gain and so much to lose and no one was worth that to me. God brought me through the worst season of my life. I suffered long and hard and I was coming out, right. I came out loving, forgiving, and releasing everybody.

"You intended to harm me, but God intended it all for good. He brought me to this position so I could save the lives of many people."
—GENESIS 50:20, NLT

Walking in forgiveness was the key to my future, my next level, and the beginning of my joyful release. Like Joseph, I understood everything that was meant for evil God intended for my good. I did not know it at the time, but I was being prepared to speak to nations, I was being prepared to write this book, I was being prepared to fulfill my destiny.

"To forgive is to set a prisoner free and discover the prisoner was you."
—LEWIS B.SMEDES

SURRENDER

"You keep track of all my sorrows. You have collected all my tears in your bottle. You have recorded each one in your book."
—PSALM 56:8, NLT

I can only imagine how many of my tears God has bottled up and recorded in His book over the last fourteen years. Writing this book has brought new tears to the surface. Some cleansed away residual pain that was still lodged deep within my soul. Most were tears of gratitude as I rehearsed how God so faithfully brought me through every test and every trial. It was only by His all sufficient grace that I was able to overcome insurmountable obstacles.

The title, *Tearful Surrender – Joyful Release* was given to me after I spent a night in tears grappling with God's will with regards to writing this book. It has taken me a period of fourteen years to live out "Tearful Surrender."

Merriman Webster defines surrender like this:

> **sur·ren·der:** 1 a: to yield to the power, control, or possession of another upon compulsion or demand b: to give up completely or agree to forgo especially in favor of another 2a: to give (oneself) up into the power of another especially as a prisoner b: to give (oneself) over to something (as an influence) intransitive senses: to give oneself up into the power of another: YIELD synonym see RELINQUISH

Surrender was given to me as a four-phase process.

- Knowing the right thing to do. Knowing God's will, (**W**hat **W**ould Jesus **D**o).

- The internal struggling, wrestling, grappling with doing the right thing.

- Submitting to doing the right thing or obeying the will of God. (Nevertheless, not my will but Yours be done.)

- The action—an action is taken. You obey or do the right thing.

A simple example:

- I know it is right to forgive those who offend me.

- My internal struggle is they caused me pain, I hurt and I do not want to forgive.

- I give in to what is right and even though it is not my desire to forgive, I will.

- The action—I forgive.

Completing the fourth step is vitally important. Isaiah 1:19 (NIV) says: "If you are willing and obedient, you will eat the good things of the land."

TEARFUL SURRENDER

It is possible to go through all four of those phases of surrender without shedding a single tear. Maybe forgiveness comes easy for you. Perhaps you can breeze through those four phases like it was nothing at all. You can forgive quickly and move on. That would be surrender, but not a tearful surrender.

Others find forgiving those who hurt them very difficult. It is hard for them to let go of the pain they feel was afflicted on them by others' actions. If you take someone who has a hard time forgiving through the same four-phase process, they are agonizing and crying crocodile tears at each phase. This is where the "tearful" part of surrender comes into play.

"They that sow (or plant) in tears will reap in joy."
—PSALM 126:5

For years I did not fully understand this passage. I thought it was my tears that were being planted that would cause me to reap in joy. The verse clearly does not say, those that sow tears will reap in joy, it says they that sow **in** tears will reap in joy. I questioned, "So what is actually being planted?"

I will use the same example I used previously. Here, the seed that is being sowed or planted in tears is "forgiveness."

- ⌘ I know it is right to forgive those who offend me *(I'm in tears)*.

- ⌘ Internally, I struggle and resist forgiving. It is hard and I am hurt *(I'm in tears)*.

- ⌘ I Surrender, even though I do not want to forgive, I will *(I'm in tears)*.

- ⌘ I forgive *(I'm in tears)*.

The four-phase process of surrender is the same as before. The outcome is the same; forgiveness. The only difference in this example and the first example is the addition of pain and emotional stress which produces tears. The result is a *Tearful Surrender.*

SOW IN TEARS

Looking back over the last fourteen year period, I have sowed many seeds that my tears have watered. My tears saturated my seeds of sorrow as I suffered one loss after another. Time and time again, I cried as I surrendered my will and my way of doing things for God's way. With many tears, I surrendered defending or speaking up for myself when I was being persecuted and falsely accused. While crying, I embarrassingly wrote my name on the offering envelope and sowed my last $1 bill. I imagine God collected an ocean full of my tears as I surrendered pride and self-reliance to Him and sowed seeds of humility. In spite of the many tears and the great losses I suffered, I never stopped sowing seeds of praise, thanksgiving, and worship to God.

God values your tears. The first occurrence of tears in the Bible is in 2 Kings 20:5, where God lets King Hezekiah know that He has heard his prayers and seen his tears. The last place in the Bible we see tears is Revelations 21:4 where God is wiping away all tears.

Surrendering in the most adverse circumstances and when it is the hardest thing to do is not just sowing in tears, it is also sowing in faith.

GOD IS FAITHFUL

The greatest lesson I learned I can put in three words: God is faithful. There are those who would have you believe that suffering is not part of the Christian experience. Being a Christian does not exempt us from life's calamities. God never promised us flowery beds of ease. Job 14:1 says, "Man that is born of a woman is of few days and full of trouble." None of us get a free pass. Pain and suffering are the great equalizers that cross social, economic, racial, and ethnic barriers. Like raindrops, pain, suffering, and grief do not discriminate. Anyone who steps outside without an umbrella when it is raining is going to get wet.

"Learning is a gift even when pain is the teacher."
—ZIG ZIGLER

In Chapter 5, I talked about the dream God gave me where I was standing on top of a high mountain, planting a dirty, tattered, war-torn American flag in victory. I had taken the territory after a long hard-fought battle. The clouds were grey, dark, and dreary. As I stood there, the scenery changed to a brilliantly bright, beautiful, sunny, cloud-filled day and I was holding a brand spanking new American flag, Ole' Glory! I had sown much in tears, now it was time to reap in joy!

A TIME FOR EVERYTHING

For everything there is a season,
a time for every activity under heaven
A time to be born and a time to die
A time to plant and a time to harvest
A time to kill and a time to heal.
A time to tear down and a time to build up
A time to cry and a time to laugh
A time to grieve and a time to dance.

—ECCLESIASTES 3:1–5 (NLT)
(Emphasis mine.)

"I know what it is to be in need, and I know what it is to have plenty.
I have learned the secret of being content in any and every situation,
whether well fed or hungry, whether living in plenty or in want."
—PHILIPPIANS 4:12, NIV

Chapter Nine

JOYFUL RELEASE

"Weeping may last through the night, but joy comes with the morning."
PSALM 30:5, NLT

One Saturday morning as I was waking up, I heard the melody to one line of a song. All I heard was, "In the morning, in the morning, it will be all over in the morning." I knew I had heard the song before, but for the life of me I could not think of any other words or who sang the song.

Later that day I was out and about running errands. I was in and out of my car and about 1:00 p.m. I jumped in the car and turned on our church's radio station, WCCD Radio 1000. To my surprise the song I heard when I woke up that morning was playing! I remembered the song when I heard it. It was entitled, *Ain't No Need To Worry* and it was recorded by Anita Baker and Marvin Winans. I listened intently to every word but what resonated in my spirit were the words, "Ain't no need to worry, what the night is gonna bring, it'll be all over in the morning." I put that line together with the line I heard earlier and I sang that melody for days.

This was no coincidence or accident, God was sending me a message that the long night season I endured was finally over and morning season had arrived. The trial was over and the purpose for my testing had been accomplished.

PURPOSE FOR THE PAIN

Joseph is my favorite Bible character and for years I have studied him. I have often looked at his life to help make sense out of mine. All that Joseph went through, the hatred of his brothers, being thrown in a pit, sold into slavery, false accusations, and his imprisonment served the purpose of preparing him for his destiny. During the thirteen years of adversity, Joseph's character was developed, strengthened, and matured.

Suffering builds character. Character is the way you think, feel, or behave. The purpose of suffering for a Christian is to build godly character; godly thoughts, feelings, and behavior. Too often, we see a person given a position or an opportunity to do something prematurely because they are gifted or favored. Their gifts or talents are able to obtain the opportunity, but it takes character to maintain. Your gifts will open doors but character will keep you in the door once you are there.

The purpose of Joseph's suffering was to prepare him for his destiny. Joseph's destiny was to save his family and preserve a nation. Everything he went through was designed by God to move him closer to the fulfillment of his destiny and to ensure he was mature when he got there.

The purpose of his suffering was not so he could have a grand palace in the suburbs of Egypt. It was not for his personal gain. It was not to obtain wealth or ride in the finest chariot, even though the position did come with an excellent benefit package. The position, power, wealth, and the influence were necessary to fulfill his destiny which was to save the lives of his family and a nation.

Like Joseph, God has made me to forget my troubles and He has made me fruitful in the place of my afflictions. The purpose of my pain was also to increase character, to humble and mature me in preparation to fulfill my destiny. I shudder as I think about the level of testing and adversity I have experienced being an indicator of the destiny I am called to walk in. I know this: the mature receive the promised inheritance and I am waiting with great expectations to see what the future holds for me.

> *"Arise, shine; for thy light is come, and the glory of the*
> *LORD is risen upon thee… the LORD shall arise*
> *upon thee, and his glory shall be seen upon thee."*
> —ISAIAH 60:1,2B

MOURNING INTO DANCING

In 2007 the Lord began telling me He was sending me to the nations. In 2011 God opened a door for me to speak at a Born to Reign conference in London, England. The trip was scheduled over the dates late in September and early October. I was ecstatic about the opportunity to speak, but more significant to me was the timing of the trip.

This was the first time in five years I was not sad during that time because I was reliving the events leading up to my husband's death. I was excited and preoccupied with preparing for the trip. October 3, the day my husband died, I was in Paris, France touring and shopping. My mourning had officially ended. October 3 the following two years, I was also out of the country in Nassau, Bahamas and Johannesburg, South Africa.

BEAUTY FOR ASHES

"To all who mourn in Israel, he will give a crown of beauty for ashes a joyous blessing instead of mourning, festive praise instead of despair."
—ISAIAH 61:3, NLT

The word I received from a stranger in December of 1999 predicted the season I walked through with great accuracy and in great detail. I was told I would see God's vindication and it would all be worth it to me then. I have seen God's vindication. I have seen so many people reap the evil they sowed in my life. Instead of gloating over their bad fortune, I prayed for them to receive God's mercy. I can say like the old song says, "Oh Lord, I know I've been changed."

Everyone who spoke against me in judgment, God has silenced. I say that for no other purpose but to say, if you allow God to fight your battles, He will. If you do the right thing, He will reward you accordingly to the cleanness of your hands in His sight. I learned that no matter how right I may have thought I was in my own eyes, this was not the standard for reward.

"I, the Lord, search all hearts and examine secret motives. I give all people their due rewards, according to what their actions deserve."
—JEREMIAH 17:10, NLT

Unequivocally and without hesitation, I can boldly say that I know God is Faithful and He is real. He can be trusted and He is true to

His Word. He is a promise keeper. He will never leave you nor will He forsake you. There was not one thing I went through that God did not allow and there was not one time He was not there. Even when I did not think He was there, He was there all the time. When it seemed like everything in my world was topsy-turvy and utter chaos, God was holding the reins.

God has blessed my life abundantly. Every defeat has become a victory. Every trial has become triumph. All things have worked together for my good because I love Him and I am called according to His purposes (Romans 8:28).

BLESSED, BROKEN, GIVEN

"And he commanded the multitude to sit down on the grass, and took the five loaves, and the two fishes, and looking up to heaven, he blessed, and brake, and gave the loaves to his disciples, and the disciples to the multitude."
—MATTHEW 14:19

The first message I ever spoke publicly was entitled, "Blessed, Broken, Given." I was nervous about speaking and I remember how long I studied and how hard I worked to meticulously lay out my message. It was a divinely inspired message and to this day, people still tell me they remember the impact it had on them.

I recently revised and delivered the message to another congregation and it was more powerful, more anointed, and more impactful than before. The message and the messenger were basically the same. The biggest difference between the first time I shared it and now was that now I had experienced the brokenness I had only read about the first time. Before I used only Bible characters as examples. This time, I could draw deeply from my own experiences as well.

The first time I had head knowledge—what I had heard or what I was told about brokenness. Now I have firsthand evidence. I had my testimony and I could say like Job, "I only heard about you before but now I have seen you with my own eyes" (Job 42:5, NLT).

If you are like me, you hate watching a good movie or reading a good book, anxiously anticipating what happens at the end and it leaves you hanging. When you started watching you didn't know it was a mini-series or there would be a sequel. I have lived the *Tearful Surrender,* and I have only just begun to live out the Joyful Release.

> *"Authentic achievement is rooted in noble desire springing from the seeds of greatness deep within the soil of your tender heart. The seeds lie dormant, seemingly lifeless, below the surface until the 'more than you can handle' pressures of life crush their outer shell releasing the 'more than enough' blueprint of your intended future into your present painful moment with a force of travail that brings them to birth.*
> —DR. MARK CHIRONNA

I have been blessed, broken, and I am now being given. *Joyful Release* will be a book all its own. I have seen glimpses of the trailer and the best is yet to come!

> *"For I reckon that the sufferings of this present time are not worthy to be compared with the glory which shall be revealed in us."*
> —ROMANS 8:18